Hundreds of Fascinating and Unique Ways to Use Your Computer

By Tina Rathbone

Edited by Gretchen Lingham
Cover illustration by Lisa Mozzini
Art direction by Leah Steward-Shahan

First Edition Copyright © 1992
Computer Publishing Enterprises
P.O. Box 23478
San Diego, CA 92193
Toll Free (800) 544-5541

0-945776-22-5
10 9 8 7 6 5 4 3 2 1

To Jan Weber and all the
quilting members of Prodigy Services.
Your kind acts express the spirit and
joy behind home computing.

Acknowledgements

My thanks to the folks at Computer Publishing Enterprises who asked me to write this book.

Thanks also to creative software publishers everywhere, who made this book possible—and necessary.

Last, but not least, I'd like to thank Maria and Andy, who are getting used to these book deadlines.

Tina Rathbone
January, 1992

Table of Contents

Foreword

For the first-time computer buyer, the initial flush of excitement can disappear all too quickly. You get home, hook up your computer, boot up the master disk or hard drive, and then. . . .

And then what?

That's always been the problem we face when buying a new home computer. Once the novelty of just having it wears off, what do you actually do with it? (Or to put it another way, how do you justify this extravagant purchase to your money-conscious husband/wife?) That's where Tina Rathbone, dressed in white like a knight of old, comes riding to the rescue. This book takes you by the hand and leads you through practical, everyday applications that not only let you use your computer for something other than doodling or games, but that simplify your life.

From balancing a checkbook or sorting recipes to developing a planting schedule for the garden, the ideas and advice found here will have a welcome place in every home.

Tina has spent countless hours reviewing and analyzing thousands of software programs (trust me; I've seen the family garage). Her lengthy experience with both the PC clone and Macintosh platforms allows her to recommend applications likely to be useful to—and usable by—the novice computer owner. Soon, like the rest of us, you'll wonder how you ever prepared your tax return, tracked your exercise program, sorted your Christmas card list or followed your stock investments without your computer.

In other words, you'll be hooked.

Jim Trageser
February, 1992

Preface

One day, several years ago, the UPS guy brought me a stack of gardening software for an article I was writing for *ComputorEdge* Magazine. The astonishment on the faces of the computer veterans around the office led me to wonder how many other types of home software existed.

This book grew out of that incident, as well as many more years of exploring this sometimes offbeat, always adventurous "other" side of computing.

Tina Rathbone

Chapter One

Household Applications

There your home computer sits, one more thing to dust. If your spouse were sitting around so idly you'd probably put him or her to work. Why not make your computer pull its weight around the house by letting it organize your life where you need it most?

Although it can't take out the garbage, your home computer can help in ways you never thought possible. Better yet, it can save you money. Best of all, it can give you more time to relax—and sit around idly yourself!

Thanks to the magic of reruns, even the youngest computer enthusiast has seen *The Jetsons*, that zippiest of celluloid Space Age families. Remember how wife/mom Jane cleaned the house by pressing a single button? Home automation software offers nearly the same level of ease and efficiency. You can pick up your car phone and punch in a code to preheat the home jacuzzi—with your home PC acting as Mission Control.

One too many jacuzzi sessions later, your heating bill has become a monthly testament to how your money's going up in smoke. Well, don't let it steam you up a minute longer. A software program that tracks utility costs, coupled with the computer's natural ability to crunch numbers, can show you where to cut energy use.

If solar panels or skylights would help, project-estimating software automates calculating the costs of such improvements.

Think these are wacky uses for a computer? That's just for starters. Right now, in your hands, you're holding the key to your home computer's usefulness. Together, this book and your computer will streamline and add fun to any part of your daily life.

Even if you live in sunny Hawaii and never give a thought to heating costs, it's a safe bet you have property insurance like the rest of us. Trouble is, before you can insure it, you have to be able to describe it. Yet tracking everything you own can be tedious and time-consuming. And who's really that organized?

Your computer, that's who! Arm it with home inventory software, and together you can log your valuables in case you ever need to replace them. Proceed with confidence (but be sure to keep a copy of the data diskette someplace off the premises).

If holidays are a time of reflection and renewal, why are there always so many last-minute details? With the right software, your computer can do everything from play carols to print greeting cards—even calculate shipping rates and delivery times, for those times when you're the DE (Designated Elf). Your computer isn't nearly as messy as a reindeer, and it won't hog up all the holiday goodies, either!

In the months leading up to New Year's, bookstores bulge with calendars that cater to every imaginable special interest. Yet home printshop software allows your computer to design and print unlimited calendars and labels—tailored to your own interests. Now you can print out an individualized calendar for each member of the family. Finicky users can even specify calendars printed out in popular "Organizer" formats, like Dayrunner.

Once the holidays are upon us, spring cleaning can't be far behind. If rearranging furniture is about the most unpleasant task you can think of, let your computer do it for you. Even though it doesn't get sweaty or cuss, it's a big help. Your computer can set down your worldly goods on a grid so you can see what goes where, before any muscles come into play.

If one look at your furnishings convinces you they're not *worth* cleaning, let alone moving, why not engage an expert to help you redecorate? Running a decorating program on your home computer will be a rewarding, hands-on learning experience. Have no fear: Your computer knows the names of all those bizarre colors. What's more, your PC will save you from having to endure a snobby decorator's disdainful sniff as he sizes up your home's *current* ambiance!

The redo is done, and you've received dozens of compliments on your home's snazzy new look. Maybe the exterior could use a little sprucing up, too. Your computer will effortlessly draft up a new addition, and calculate the cost and quantities of materials you need, to boot.

What about the four-footed, winged, or finned contingent? Your loving pets are part of the family, too. Learn how to keep them healthy and happy by using your computer.

Then there's that other four-footed breed, the gas guzzling variety (known more for being man's worst friend than his best). Even your home PC can't make an oil change seem fun. But taking care of your car or RV can become less of an ordeal when your computer organizes the details. You may learn a few things, too.

This is the only nation on Earth where companies offer you money, in the form of cents-off coupons, to try out their products. Yet collecting coupons (and remembering you have them) is too often seen as a time-wasting hassle. Your computer can organize those coupons and rebates for you, once it's loaded with coupon database software.

And, if you're in the market for a home, Chapter Two describes Home Mortgage software that helps you calculate payments, tells you whether you should wait or plunge in, and even figures a pre-payment rate that shaves years off your mortgage.

Tasks for Household Applications Software

- Home Automation
- Charting Home Energy Costs
- Logging Home Inventories
- Helping Out Around the Holidays
- Printing Calendars and Labels
- Moving Furniture, Interior Decorating and Home Design
- Learning About and Enjoying Family Pets
- Maintaining Autos and Recreational Vehicles
- Organizing and Tracking Manufacturer's Coupons

Home Automation

Imagine yourself driving home from work one fall evening. You note with relief that the gridlock's no worse than usual. Slowly, your mind wanders from the bumper two feet ahead to the evening ahead. You feel a sudden urge to soak in your hot tub.

Grabbing the cellular car phone, you call your house, where an electronic answering system politely requests an access code before further conversation can take place. After punching in some numbers, you add some others that tell your circuited servant to start heating the hot tub. Almost as an afterthought, you command it to phone you back when the tub reaches a toasty 104 degrees.

Suddenly you remember you had other plans for the evening: The gang's coming over for a few games of pool. Quickly, you phone your bit-based butler and cancel the jacuzzi. Instead, you tell it to start the dishwasher (you'll need plenty of clean mugs) and crank the heater in the basement rec room.

As you pull into the driveway, a sound sensor tells your computer to turn on the yard lights and prepare for a visitor. Simultaneously, a dog's bark is activated. Smiling, you deactivate the electronic pooch and prepare to show your friends the wonders of an automated household tonight. "Now if only I could figure a way to rig that pool table," you think.

What does your home PC do all day when you're away? With a home automation software package called *Dynasty,* your PC can be the control center of every electronic function in your home.

Ordinary lights and appliances go on and off on an automatic schedule for that "lived-in look" that discourages burglars. With distance extenders, *Dynasty* can watch over your property and respond to any intrusion with verbal warnings, alarm sirens or by placing phone calls to family, neighbors, police or fire departments. *Dynasty* can control every operation of your TV, VCR and audio system, so you'll never have to struggle with VCR programming again!

Dynasty answers your phone, takes messages and can respond to spoken commands using voice recognition. Even heating and air conditioning is under your computer's control, for optimum comfort and energy savings. *Dynasty*'s scope of involvement in your life is entirely up to you. This customizeable software can turn your home into a simple, controlled system or a techno-mecca to rival the Starship Enterprise—depending on add-ons you select from a formidable list including infrared, analog input, relay output, voice synthesis and wireless security.

The foremost considerations in a home automation software system are expandability and flexibility. Can you add features as your interests (and finances) grow? Also, how difficult is the system to install and maintain? Be sure to hire your friendly electrician to install wiring and other potentially dangerous fixtures. There's a limit to do-it-yourselfing; even rewiring a lamp can be hazardous if you don't turn off all the circuits first.

Charting Home Energy Costs

Your computer can save you money by telling you how much you're spending to heat or cool your house. *Home Utility Recorder* for the IBM-compatible family of computers asks you to enter your monthly utility bills. The program averages the cost, and gives you a detailed analysis of where your energy dollars are going.

After looking over the computer's report, you may decide to add solar panels. A program called *Telisolar* will help determine the cost effectiveness of such a project. Any remodeling projects you then decide on will be based on intelligent comparison.

If you decide that a remodeling project is for you, a program called *Homeowner* will organize the renovation and save you money. Don't rely solely on the contractor's figures. Let your computer be your remodeling consultant.

Home Inventory/Household Records Software

You know you should get organized and record serial numbers, etc., of all your possessions. But the task seems too tedious. Don't wait until a fire or theft makes conducting a household inventory impossible. *Homeventory* for the IBM-compatible family of computers creates an inventory of your home and its contents. Inventory programs have you list your possessions in categories or "rooms." Most come with rooms already defined, plus ones you can customize to meet the configuration of your own house. For

```
xxxxxx   Add an Item   xxxxxx   (To exit, enter blanks, choose M )

      Residence: John Q. Public
        Address: 123 Main St., Anytown, USA
           Room: Living Room
        Item #:  1
xxx Type ONLY within [ ] brackets xxx   Press Enter for next field
    Description: [Stereo                                  ]
  Purchase Date: [12/25/89] mm/dd/yy
 Purchase Price: [2,500.00   ] dddddd.cc
Place Purchased: [Wow Stereo                              ]
  Serial Number: [123423            ]
      Other I.D.: [                                       ]
   Other Info 1: [                                        ]
   Other Info 2: [                                        ]
```

Household inventory programs keep records of your possessions.

the items in each room, you enter descriptions, prices, purchase date, serial numbers or other identification. You then get a detailed list of your valuables, either for insurance records or just to gloat over how much neat stuff you've accumulated.

Crisp graphics like those found on *Household Goods Inventory Management Program* make the whole process more enjoyable.

All programs of this type let you add, modify or delete values whenever you want. You can print out the inventory room by room or once for the whole house.

Most programs let you sort, list and print possessions by various categories: *Asset Tracking System* even lets you sort by manufacturer, in case that third Black & Decker food processor you got for a wedding present catapults you into rebate-heaven. Be they ever so humble, your possessions will enjoy being catalogued by you and your computer.

Holiday Applications

When spirits are high and everyone's having fun, why not involve your computer in the festivities? Programs for your computer can play holiday sounds; print cards, wrapping paper and holiday letters; or teach you and your family more about a holiday's meaning and origin.

For Apple and IBM computers, programs from Davka in the *All About* series feature comprehensive guides to customs and practices of Chanukah, Passover, Purim, and other holy days. *Christmas Sampler* from Cross Educational Software illustrates "The Night Before Christmas" and "The Christmas Story," and plays 12 carols. Another program from the same publisher called *Christmas Story* teaches the Biblical version of Christ's birth.

Some people know that being organized is the key to making it through the holidays without going insane. Such a person is Sue Robichaux. Sue developed a holiday database called *Ornament Master*. It lets you log ornaments by description, price, date acquired, and notes. The program offers a Christmas card list that prints labels, a shopping list that you can print by store, a party list and more. With registration, this shareware package comes with a printed, bound manual and a wider range of print functions. Absent-minded gift buyers will quickly recognize the benefits of being able to sort and print a gift list by store: no more backtracking through holiday hordes of crazed shoppers.

Hard-core gift givers will love a shipping tracker called *Pony Express (PE)*. *PE* calculates shipping rates and projects delivery times for letters and packages via UPS or the post office. The programmers update it after each new rate increase, and figure in rates for express mail; first, second, and third class; second-day Air and more. *PE*'s best feature: When you already know postage rates, you can drop packages into the mailbox instead of standing in the unbearable holiday lines.

If you've racked your brain, but inspiration is as hazy as the LA skyline, try *Gifts*. The program suggests gifts based on the amount you want to spend, recipient's age, sex and interests.

Calendar Programs/Label Design

Even though this is the age of the paperless home office, sometimes a wall calendar still comes in handy. But as they fill up with duties and appointments, your typical, puny wall calendar can get awfully hard to read. Nobody makes calendars with big enough date blanks for all your family's activities.

Your home computer can change all that. Special calendar-making programs let you design your own daily, weekly, monthly, bi-weekly, or whatever calendars.

Each family member can dream up calendars that suit any hobby or club they're into. Young children will get a better grasp of organizing time once they sit down and enter all their commitments. And you can hang specialized calendars where they'll do the most good—a gardening calendar inside a potting shed or garage, for example.

Calendar programs come with every sort of font and graphic imaginable. They even speak foreign languages, as in the program *Calendarmate*, which prints in French, German and Spanish. You can usually import graphics in the more popular formats, too. Print out appointments or regularly scheduled meetings right along with the calendar, or leave the dates blank and fill them in with a pencil —the low-tech way.

Is your kitchen spice cabinet bulging with unidentifiable bottles of green herbs or golden powders? Sure, *you* know what's in there, but unless someone else can figure it out, dinners cooked by other members of the family are going to taste pretty bland. Computer software that designs and prints labels can identify all sorts of things around the house. You'll never have to search for disk labels again—or any kind of label, for that matter. Equipped with label-maker software, your home computer can slap a name on anything: video tapes, files, even your kids' friends.

Most label-making software lets you specify the dimensions of the label you want, along with type sizes and orientation. You can print multiple copies of a label just by pressing one key with *Labels Unlimited*'s "ditto" feature. Similar programs let you print sequentially-numbered labels—good for inventory and archive purposes. Make sure the program runs with your printer.

Interior Decoration/Furniture Moving Software

Ah, publishing terminology is a wondrous thing. Now they've given a special name to the food/home/lifestyle magazines: Shelter Books. Whatever the name, they're full of inspirational photos of sublime homes where perfect, tidy beings reside. Did you ever pick up a "shelter" magazine and wonder just how those lovely rooms

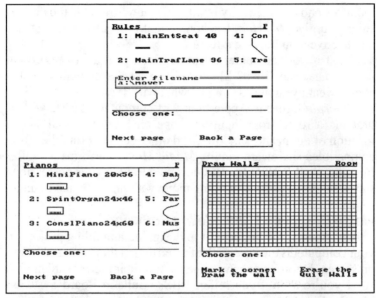

Furniture-moving with a computer saves your back!

got that way? Your computer already knows! Budding home decorators will enjoy two programs from Abracadata: *Instant Decorator* and *Design Your Own Home: Interiors.*

Based on the Two-Seasons Design method, *Instant Decorator* asks you to classify each of your major furnishings in terms of its "seasonal characteristics." Objects aren't the only elements with seasonal characteristics: spacing and arrangement have them, too. The program teaches you how to blend two seasons harmoniously and make sure nothing you buy in the future ever clashes with your neat new look. Learning this system will give you a solid foundation for future decorating enterprises (and might help you dress nicer, too). The program comes with nifty color charts for each season (bet you can't tell summer from winter).

The other program lets you move little pictures of furniture around in a room you specify until it seems pleasing. *Design Your Own Home: Interiors* gives you an easy-to-use interface and has a versatile graphics program built in. The program supports color monitors and automatically builds side views from the top dimensions you give. *Interiors* lets you look at rooms from almost any perspective—an important feature.

What if your computer could help you plan a move before a single piano was lifted? Many software packages will save you some sweat by showing you just what will fit where.

Floorplan, for the Apple family of computers, assists you by drawing a room from input you give on room size and shape, location of doors and windows, and other details. From the IBM-compatibles shareware family, *Magic Mover* performs a similar function. And *BDL.Move* was designed to help your possessions survive either an office or home move without too much trauma.

Home Design and Remodeling Software

Undeniably, the big benefit to designing a building project on your computer is the way you're forced to first think things through on screen, before expensive experts start their meters running.

If you're a do-it-yourselfer, BBSs (Bulletin Board Systems) like Prodigy feature expensive experts who hang around on-line dispensing advice for free. (Actually, for the cost of your monthly membership—around $12 per month last time I checked). Remember, measure twice, cut once! (Your computer is real good at these measurement types of things. . . .)

A host of programs like *Kitchen*, *Floorplan* or *Dream House Professional* enable you to be the architect you've always wanted to be. Look for pull-down menus, varied printer fonts, and ready-made icons representing things like toilets and sinks in *Floorplan* and other programs from ComputerEasy. Before you buy, you'll want to check the side of the software box to ensure that the program's compatible with your printer, too.

Concrete quantities, framing materials, windows, stucco, roofing, and more can be pinpointed with a program called, simply, *Home*. *PC-Estimator* includes built-in data for material, labor and equipment rates, fully customizable. *Remodel Estimator* offers a cost database and a report generator. It has a built-in calculator, and several estimate samples for miscellaneous remodeling jobs, like the bathroom, kitchen, garage and more.

Maybe you think on a smaller scale—an HO-gauge scale, to be exact. A program called *Hometown, U.S.A.* lets you design and print out buildings for your model railroad setup or your racing car outfit. Winner of the Software Publishing Association's "Creativity Program of the Year" Excellence in Software award, this program enables you to be master of your own world. Design it, print it, paint it, fold it and there you go. The buildings can also be used as tree ornaments, place cards, gift boxes or models for the house of your dreams. How about creating a ghost town for your "antique" Barbie dolls, or an underground hangout for the Teenage Mutant Ninja Turtles?

Pet Your Computer

Use your computer and a modem to call the pet experts on the Prodigy On-Line service. Weekly "columns" hand out advice on subjects of interest to any pet owner. And pet-oriented bulletin boards, whether on Prodigy or right in your home town, are an excellent way to meet fellow animal lovers.

Any pet owner can relate to the necessity of tracking pet vaccinations. *Med Pet* comes with the most popular dog and cat vaccination types already loaded; you can add additional shots and schedule them, too. The program prints a list for each pet.

A difficult but rewarding task is tracing your pet's lineage. For horse lovers, there's *Horses*, a shareware program that maintains pedigree records for horse breeders. This program includes registry numbers and charts to five generations. Dog lovers will enjoy *Pedigree*, which keeps track of AKC awards and pedigrees. You can trace line-breeding and produce lists of descendants and other pertinent statistics.

Automate Auto Maintenance

A good auto maintenance program should remind you when it's time for that oil change. They all do, once you run the software. It's a Catch 22 situation: Unless the program is memory resident (and none are, to my knowledge), it must be booted up before it can tell you to mind your car. Apart from this drawback, a program called *Chris's Automobile Recorder* is excellent for logging and tracking automotive events such as monthly checkups, oil changes, fuel fill-ups and major repairs.

You can sort for a report of the current state of your car, and see, printed out if you like, figures on fuel economy, oil consumption, mileage and operating costs—updated daily, automatically showing the date. You can view any repair, purchase or other event in detail. Can't remember what to tell the guy at the shop? *CAR* lets you print out an inspection form to take with you. The best feature is a Preventative Maintenance Due screen, complete with pop-up windows and color-keyed entries (red for overdue, etc.). The full-screen help menus and easy interface, as well as its simple good looks and $7 price tag, gives this one a guaranteed place on my hard drive.

Motorhome Manager helps you track RV supplies, maintenance schedules, and everything else you need to vacation in safety and comfort. You can use the program with cabins and houseboats, too.

Coupon and Refund Software

Many people consider manufacturer's cents-off coupons too much of a bother, so they end up missing out on real savings—especially in stores that offer double coupon refunds. People who scoff at coupon redemption probably wouldn't mind getting a 66-percent raise when review time rolls around at work. Yet, if you double a dollar-off coupon and deduct that $2 from a $3 deodorant, you've just earned two-thirds more money.

Your home computer loves to organize you. Why not leave the tedium of sorting coupons to the computer? This type of software often comes with a database feature to track expiration dates, saving you possible embarrassment in the checkout line.

Homing in on Home Software

After reading about the dozens of practical, unexpected home applications around, you're probably thinking "There must be more." And you're right! Shareware catalogs, BBSs and on-line services are teeming with other sources and ideas for ways to improve life around the house with your computer. Enjoy, and write me if you find new uses that should go into subsequent editions of this book!

Sources for Household Applications Software

Remember, prices in the world of computer software change rapidly. Prices listed here were accurate at the writing of this book, but don't be surprised if they've changed soon after.

Home Automation
Dynasty Software
($395 with three free X-10 hardware modules; IBM-compatibles)
Home Automation Laboratories, 5500 Highland Parkway, Suite 450
Atlanta GA 30082, (800) HOME-LAB, (404) 319-6000
Call for a nifty, free catalog of home automation goodies.

Home PC Applications
Home PC Applications Library
($49.95 for 100 programs; IBM-compatibles)
EMS Professional Shareware Libraries, 4505 Buckhurst Court
Olney, MD 20832, (301) 924-3594
The folks at EMS have gathered more than 100 home applications that fall into most of the categories in this chapter (and many more). A front-end menu makes evaluating, decompressing and running these programs easy.

Charting Home Energy Costs
Home Utility Recorder
($10, IBM-compatibles, Macintosh)
Heizer Software, 1941 Oak Park Blvd., Suite 30
Pleasant Hill, CA 94523, (415) 943-7667

Telisolar, 4th Edition
($59.95, IBM-compatibles)
Tesseract Enterprises, Ltd., 4334 140th Street
Savage, MN 55378, (612) 894-9378

Homeowner ($64.95, IBM-compatibles)
Dynacomp, Inc., 178 Phillips Road
Webster, NY 14580, (716) 265-4040

PC-Estimator ($8)
Home ($35)
Available through popular shareware outlets, including
Public Brand Software, (800) 426-DISK.

Home Inventory/Household Records Software
Homeventory
($24.95; Apple, Commodore 64/128, IBM-compatibles)
Zephyr Services, 1900 Murray Avenue
Pittsburgh, PA 15208, (412) 422-6600

Home Insurance Inventory ($29.95, IBM-compatibles)
Dynacomp, Inc., 178 Phillips Road
Webster, NY 14580, (716) 265-4040

Household Goods Inventory Management Program ($10)
M.J. Cloutier, 591-B Michelson Road
Monterey, CA 93940
(Also available as part of the EMS *Home PC Library*)

Asset Tracking System ($10)
Garrett A. Keel, 1228 30th Street South
Milwaukee, WI 53215
(Also available as part of the EMS *Home PC Library*)

Holiday Applications
Christmas Sampler ($15)
Christmas Story ($15) (IBM-compatibles)
Cross Educational Software, 504 E. Kentucky Ave.
Ruston, LA 71270, (318) 255-8921

Christmas Concert Vols 1 & 2
(Disks #1211, 1212; IBM-compatibles)
PC-SIG, 1030 East Duane Avenue, Suite D
Sunnyvale, CA 94086, (800) 245-6717 (USA), (408) 730-9291

Hyperseder ($39.95)
Vezot Hatorah ($39.95)
(Many more, write for catalog; Macintosh)
Davka Corp., 845 N. Michigan Ave., Suite 843
Chicago, IL 60611, (800) 621-8227

Ornament Master ($10, IBM-compatibles)
Sue Robichaux, P.O. Box 91016-199
Baton Rouge, LA 70821
(Also available as part of the EMS *Home PC Library*)

Pony Express ($50, IBM-compatibles)
Available through popular shareware outlets, including
Public Brand Software, (800) 426-DISK.

Gifts ($10, IBM-compatibles)
Available through popular shareware outlets, including
.Public Brand Software, (800) 426-DISK.

15

Giftwrap ($15, IBM-compatibles)
Available through popular shareware outlets, including
Public Brand Software, (800) 426-DISK.

Label Makers/Calendar Programs
Labels Unlimited ($69.95, IBM-compatibles)
Power Up, Channelmark Corporation, 2929 Campus Drive
San Mateo, CA 94403, (800) 851-2917, (800) 223-1479 (in CA)

Mr. Label ($29, IBM-compatibles)
Available through popular shareware outlets, including
Public Brand Software, (800) 426-DISK.

Calendar Creator Plus ($69.95, IBM-compatibles)
Power Up, Channelmark Corporation, 2929 Campus Drive
San Mateo, CA 94403, (800) 851-2917, (800) 223-1479 (in CA)

Calendarmate ($22, IBM-compatibles)
Available through popular shareware outlets, including
Public Brand Software, (800) 426-DISK.

Home Design and Remodeling Software
The Instant Decorator ($49.95)
Design Your Own Home: Interiors ($49.95)
Design Your Own Home: Architecture ($49.95)
Design Your Own Home: Landscape ($49.95)
(Apple IIs, Macintosh, IBM-compatibles)
Abracadata, P.O. Box 2440
Eugene, OR 97402, (800) 451-4871, (503) 342-3030

Magic Mover ($3.95/disk, IBM-compatibles)
Pan World International, P.O. Box 714
Campbell, CA 95009

BDL.Move ($39.95, IBM-compatibles)
BDL Homeware, 2509 N. Campbell, Suite 328M
Tucson, AZ 85719, (602) 577-1435

Floorplan ($49.95)
Dream House Professional ($69.95, IBM-compatibles)
ComputerEasy, 414 East Southern Road
Tempe, AZ 85282, (602) 829-9614, (800) 522-3279

PC-Estimator ($89)
Home ($35)
Remodel Estimator ($99, IBM-compatibles)
Available through popular shareware outlets, including
Public Brand Software, (800) 426-DISK.

Hometown, U.S.A. ($39.95, IBM-compatibles, Macintosh)
Publishing International, 22014 7th Avenue South
Seattle, WA 98198, (206) 824-0656

Pet Software
Med Pet ($10)
A.R. McGall Jr., 8970 Fenner Road
Baldwinsville, NY 13027
(Also available as part of the EMS *Home PC Library*)

Horses ($35)
Pedigree ($40, IBM-compatibles)
Available through popular shareware outlets, including
Public Brand Software, (800) 426-DISK.

Auto Maintenance Software
Chris' Automobile Recorder ($7, IBM-compatibles)
Cooney Applied Technology, P.O. Box 292039
Kettering, OH 45429-0039
(Also available as part of the EMS *Home PC Library*)

Motorhome Manager ($50, IBM-compatibles)
Available through popular shareware outlets, including
Public Brand Software, (800) 426-DISK.

Coupon and Refund Software
Coupon Organizer
($39.95, Apple, IBM-compatibles)
Andent, Inc., 1000 North Avenue
Waukegan, IL 60085, (708) 223-5077

Chapter Two

Personal and Household Finance Software

People who use computers in their business wouldn't think of calculating cash flow with a paper and pencil. Instead, they boot up a spreadsheet and use the computer's power and speed to figure out whether they're making any money. Yet folks with a computer at home rarely take advantage of their computer's tireless ability to crunch numbers.

Of course, most businesses use powerhorse spreadsheets and databases to track profit and loss. Home users who just want to get a handle on their bank balance would never want or need all the features crammed into programs like Microsoft *Excel* or *dBASE V*. Fortunately, the variety and convenience of personal and household finance software makes it possible to stay in the black without ever reaching for one of the biggies.

Whether you balance a checkbook once a month or play the stock market with nerves of steel, computer software can help you get—and stay—organized. Besides giving you the feeling that you're getting more use out of your home computer, personal finance software can save you time and maybe even money.

A note of caution: Back up your data often. These are your financial records. Computers are subject to mechanical failures, so back up your work—preferably twice—and keep one set somewhere else altogether. End of sermon.

__Please Note:__ Financial and legal advice is by no means implied by the contents of this chapter, or this book. The services of a professional should be sought in situations involving investments, financial management and bequests. The author and publisher assume no liability for problems arising from the use of personal computers and/or software in personal financial management.

Tasks for Personal Finance Software

- Track and Write Checks
- Pay Bills Automatically
- Assess Earnings and Financial Goals
- Log Important Records
- Organize and Pay Taxes
- Monitor Real Estate Holdings
- Evaluate Loans
- Watch Stock Market Investments
- Log Business Expenses
- Assess Health Insurance

Checkbook Software

Keeping track of a checking account means more than throwing your statements into a file folder with the vague vow to "get around to that reconciliation soon." Whether you've given up entirely on seeing the numbers balance, or you do it faithfully once a month and know there must be an easier way, there's a checkbook balancing software program to fit your needs.

While most integrated financial management programs feature a checking account manager, they offer a total solution you might not want. If simple checkbook management is all you need, buy a program that does just that.

Checkbook management programs can track your check register; some can generate reports and spreadsheets. Several checkbook software programs will print the check you've just logged when you feed in printer check forms, available by special-order. Look for checking software that can track recurring payments, like a car payment, the rent, or a student loan repayment.

If you keep more than one checking account, look for a program that can keep up with you. *Andrew Tobias' Checkwrite Plus* forces you to be disciplined by assigning each payment to a category. This level of prep-work may seem tedious, but the records you end up with are a godsend at tax time.

Imagine being able to pay bills electronically without ever having to mail a single envelope. Electronic checking systems like *CheckFree* make it easy to stay organized—for a price. Besides paying bills, the program oversees routine banking, budgeting, and funds management—electronically. An automated check register tracks payment activity and record keeping. *CheckFree* spits out reports automatically, so you can stay updated on income, budget, and expenditures. This program handles recurring bills, too.

Drawbacks? Although the convenience may be worthwhile if you live in a remote setting, *CheckFree* entails a one-time software/subscription cost plus a monthly fee (for up to 20 transactions). If you pay 20 bills a month, you can probably afford *CheckFree*. (Then again, maybe that means you *can't* afford *CheckFree*.) You'll also need a modem and communications software that, teamed with *CheckFree*, will let you conduct your transactions directly with the Federal Reserve.

Financial Management Software

Financial management software tries to cover a lot of ground. If you're really dedicated and organized to begin with, it succeeds in its goal to be a total financial solution. This type of computer program takes the basic function of checkbook management and expands it into every realm of personal and home finance. You get an investment counselor, financial advisor and bookkeeper for one low price—and it won't want to "do lunch" as often.

Although this book is not intended as a review of individual software packages, detailed descriptions are offered of the leading applications in various categories to give you an idea of features you'll want to keep in mind.

In general, however, when used diligently a financial management program should be able to keep track of your checkbook and credit cards, as well as determine how much insurance you should carry, estimate your federal income taxes, and set up your children's college fund.

Databases handling these various financial areas are usually linked, supplying reports of one or all of the parts that make up your financial picture.

Sales/AR							
LEARNED LUMBER CO. For the month of February, 1987				Debits	Credits		
Date	Description	Invoice#	Account#	Invoice Amount	Sales/Tax Amount	S T	T C
02/19	Cement Mix - 50 Bags/ A8899	23130	1050/0400	500.00			

	Employees			
50/ Bags Cement Mix	LEARNED LUMBER CO. For the month of February, 1987			
02/25 190 6 by 8 - (5 Foot)				
190/ 6 by 8 5 Foot Length				
02/26 Nails, Plywood and Doors	ID	Pay Type	Employee Name	Social Security #
50/ Boxes, #10 Nails	1000	SALR	Brown, John J.	465-99-3567
30/ Door Frames	1050	SALR	Carson, John T.	111-22-3456
400/ Sheets 3/4" Plywood	1100	HOUR	David, Sam R.	342-54-7738

Checking-CRJ						
LEARNED LUMBER CO. For the month of February, 1987				Total this Batch		
Date	Net Amt of Deposit	Received From/Description	Ref	Account#	D b	Amount	T C
	' '	6.5% Sales Tax	Feb Wk 2	2015		117.00
02/16	6163.16	Cash Sales	Feb Wk 3	4030/01		5592.00
	' '	Cash Sales	Feb Wk 3	4030/02		195.00
	' '	6.5% Sales Tax	Feb Wk 3	2015		376.16
02/23	260.93	Cash Sales	Feb Wk 4	4030/01		200.00

Financial software keeps you out of the red.

A good financial program should help you set up a budget without too much trouble. Your investments should be easy to track. A good feature to look for is the ability to calculate your net worth. It's best to shop for the program that has features you think you'll use, because the high-end financial management programs can run into several hundred dollars.

Intuit's best-selling *Quicken* program for Apple, IBM-compatible, and Macintosh computers can keep separate cash, credit card, and asset/liability accounts; preset home and business accounts with flags for tax items; print out longhand amounts in several check printing formats; perform automatic credit card reconciliation and payment; generate several reports, such as tracking tax-related items or travel expenses; and compare actual figures to a pre-programmed budget. Regular upgrades to this software guarantee that investment tracking and other advanced features will enhance whatever version is current. The software has won numerous awards.

Users acclaim Andrew Tobias' *Managing Your Money* for its thoroughness. A word processor even lurks within the program.

With the latest hopped-up version of *Windows*, Microsoft Corporation has almost guaranteed its bid for world domination. Considering that financial management programs head the home software top-ten consistently, it was just a matter of time before Gilligan-look-alike Bill Gates, Microsoft's richest-man-in-the-USA CEO, saw the potential in personal finance programs and came out with one to run under his *Windows* DOS-shell.

Microsoft *Money* is, above all else, flexible. It imports/exports files in the *Quicken* QIF format so you can make the transition easily to this software. *Money* (award for blunt product name of the year) links directly with *TurboTax* and *Tax Cut*, best-sellers in their categories, so you don't have to bother with cut-and-paste.

The usual features apply here: deposits and withdrawals; recurring payments; automatic reconciliation; credit card activity; advance warning on future transaction due dates; categorized expense tracking, sortable by payee, type, project, client, property and date; and investment tracking.

Money prints out reports, summaries and budgets in as many flavors as you decide. And the net worth report is always good for a few laughs.

Pluses? The manual's well done; it even lists command shortcuts on the back cover. And if you just can't get the blasted account to balance, crafty *Money* even includes an option to let it hunt for errors in the reconciliation process. Choose the SmartReconcile feature and the program searches for a transaction that contains a misplaced decimal point or transposed digits. At least it asks you before it changes the math! Do you write checks to the same parties over and over? A feature called SmartFill takes over typing a payee name once the first few letters are recognized. It fills in last amount paid, category and memo, too. Then you can edit the entry to suit today's particulars. Handy!

Drawbacks? The box is stuffed with offers for add-on "essentials" like pre-printed blank checks (50 for $8.95, gasp!) and personalized sticky notes.

After you've marveled ("What went wrong!") at your net worth, it's a good idea to record all the whats, wheres, and whos in one place. Keep handy your essential data on bank accounts, monthly bills, pensions, insurance policies, tax records, property holdings, and medical records with a program for IBM-compatibles called *For the Record*.

This program features a question-and-answer session module that gently guides you into confessing where the good silver is hidden. *For the Record*'s manual discusses estate planning, taxes, legal records and more. You can't take it with you, but *For the Record* lets you tell others where it is.

Will Software

Speaking of taking it with you (and we must, eventually, consider this circumstance, no matter how much we'd like to avoid it): You already know you can't take it with you, but do you know who you're going to leave it to? Will-writing software forces you to organize your last requests.

The latest edition of *WillMaker* from Nolo Press features a well-planned illustrated manual that discusses everything from providing for a pet to naming a guardian for your children. It tells about gifts, living trusts, joint tenancy and other alternatives. It even gives pointers on how to hire a decent lawyer in case you need one (alone worth the price of the software).

On-screen help is ever ready and refers back to the manual for more detailed info. The screens are full of visual cues and questions that take you through a simple will in about 15 minutes.

A program called *WillPower* offers a worksheet with which you can figure your net worth—it gets you thinking about what you have before asking who'll get it. *WillPower*'s manual details alternatives to wills, and gives a legal rundown on each state, as well as an on-screen glossary.

Drawbacks: The help menu bombards you with every possible topic, unlike *WillMaker*, which is context-sensitive. Worse, *WillPower*'s opening screen tells you to read the manual before attempting to make your will. This scares off the average user. It would be wise if this program encouraged initial exploration of the program with gradual dips into the manual.

If living trusts seem to fit your situation better than a will, Nolo Press also makes a living trust program, *Nolo's Living Trust*, currently for the Macintosh platform. Nolo also publishes legal self-help books on dozens of topics. It's best to send away for a catalog.

It's Legal creates wills, power of attorney, leases, promissory notes and other legal documents, if variety is what you're seeking. The screen looks rather busy and hard to read, however.

Personal Law Firm generates 30 nasty-looking documents, including a will.

> ***Please note:*** *Computer-generated wills are null and void in the State of Louisiana.*

Credit Repair Software

You have a right to see your credit rating. And if you're contemplating a big purchase, like a home, check out your current standing before your mortgage company does. You may find more than a few surprises lurking there.

A program called *The Credit Report Repair Kit* can help you see where you stand. Based on a step-by-step plan to repair or establish credit, the program uses the same techniques as credit attorneys. (If you're really in bad shape, go see a professional, of course. But run the program ahead of time to prepare for the visit. Most professionals charge hourly rates, and if you're prepared you'll save time and money.)

Each time the screen updates itself, you'll see a different financial hint or trick at the bottom. The program contains addresses and phone numbers for the major credit rating companies, easing the whole process enormously.

Tax Software

Taxes. Sigh. No matter how prepared you think you are, there's always some essential information you can't locate at the last minute. Fortunately, many of the financial management programs already discussed in this chapter help you do tax planning earlier in the year, before it's too late. For the actual tax return session, however, you'll want a tax preparation software package.

With the help of tax preparation software, your computer can help organize all the random bits of data into a meaningful 1040 form. Many tax programs work in conjunction with the financial management software programs and checkbook organizers mentioned above, so your data is already semi-organized. The beauty of tax programs is that, once entered, data is automatically entered on every significant line of the tax return.

One feature to look for is the simultaneous preparation of your state and federal returns. The better programs come with blank tax forms acceptable to the IRS, so your computer and printer work in tandem to produce a flawless, eraser-dust-free tax return. Make sure the program you select offers automatic cross-checking of your input against data previously entered, to prevent mistakes. Several help screens are essential, as are IRS instruction screens that can be accessed when you need them.

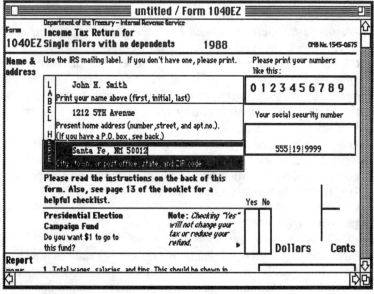

Income tax software forces you to get organized, while eliminating duplicate data entries.

Real Estate Software

It used to be that one of the fastest paths to riches (besides choosing wealthy parents) was real estate. Although that's not as true as it was in the booming '80s, a good real estate software package can help you evaluate a property to make sure that fixer-upper doesn't become a downer.

Most real estate management programs project rental income, in case you decide to become a land baron. Expenses, financing, cash flows, taxes, and resale values are all features you should look for in a real estate program. Also desirable is the ability to figure adjustable and fixed-rate mortgages and depreciation.

RealData publishes a range of high-end real estate programs written for the Macintosh family of computers. Its *Property Management* I & II series can do everything for you if you own income property except keep those rent checks coming in on time. (That part can't be enforced by any software program I know of!) The program features a detailed property profile, tenant statements, a cash receipts and disbursements journal, check printing, chart of accounts' financial statements, and much more.

Loan Software

Shopping for a loan can be a headache. Loan officers want you to feel they're doing you some kind of favor, when in fact they're *selling* you a service—a very expensive service, I might add. So where's their service-mindedness?

Before you undergo even one step of what is going to be a huge ordeal, why not let your home computer figure the preliminary round of numbers? Many software programs out there can evaluate interest, fees, points and more. A good loan evaluation software package will let you save various loan calculations to disk for comparison. You can use a spreadsheet to get the same results, but with these specialized programs, you just plug in the numbers. Programs are available for different types of loans, as well. How much will that new car *really* cost you?

Lassen Software's *Loan Manager* solves for any loan variable, so you can save money when shopping for credit. It solves for the unknown when presented with any three of four common loan parameters: amount, term, interest, and payment. Individual loans can be named and saved to disk for later retrieval. Reports can be output to printer or saved as an ASCII file. The manual is friendly and the help screens useful.

Zephyr Software offers *Finance Super*, which will do just about any financial calculation.

A Winning Strategy

"Advance payments of $25 per month will save a family with a $75,000 home loan more than $34,000 in interest, and more than five years of mortgage payments."

"On the typical $2,000 credit card balance, $25 a month, in addition to the minimum required payment, will save over $6,000, and more than 28 years."

These startling facts come to you courtesy of Good Advice Press, publishers of *The Banker's Secret* book and software program. Many people fail to realize how much money they could save on their mortgages if they were to add the price of a good lunch out to their payment. Prepayment is one of those secret financial tricks the guy in the BMW next to you at the stoplight knows. *Banker's Secret* helps you figure out how many thousands you can save with monthly prepayments. The best deal is the complete package, which comes with a book explaining the finer points of the prepayment strategy, plus both the mortgage and credit card programs.

Best of all, when you buy the software you get sample copies of the *Banker's Secret Bulletin* newsletter, full of tips on pinching pennies (so you can use those pennies to pay off your mortgage sooner!). I wish space would permit me to print excerpts here.

Authors Marc Eisenson and Nancy Castleman deserve the "Home Software Heroes" award for enabling self-empowerment and smarter living through home computing!

Stock Market Software

Investing in the stock market can be risky, but the power of your home computer can help lessen that risk by keeping you organized. Portfolio management is easy with your computer's database capabilities, while your computer's spreadsheet can calculate the bottom line in a second. Many smaller programs are available to help you figure it all out.

High-end stock market programs are actually tied to on-line stock market databases that you access with your modem. These give you minute-by-minute updates. Hopefully, you're adept at the ins and outs of the market if you subscribe to the on-line databases, because fees run into hundreds of dollars per month. But even reasonably priced programs like *Fundgraf* for IBM-compatible computers produce stock market reports and can graph and analyze funds or stocks.

Expense Logs

Although this book deals mainly with home uses for computers, the line between business and personal finances can sometimes blur. Do you ever travel for your company or home business? If the answer is "yes," you may welcome the convenience and efficiency of an expense log software program.

Programs like *Expense Master* for the IBM-compatible family of computers can create reports for nonbillables, billable jobs, personal expenses, year-to-date expenses, credit cards, meals, entertainment, and other expenses. Reports can be custom-tailored to your fussy accounting department's standards.

Expense Master will let you enter your expenses in any order. This means that as you're pulling little bits of paper with numbers scrawled on them from your pockets and suitcase lining, you can run over to the computer and enter them into the software program. Voila! The program sorts the totals by category and date, and calculates everything. *Expense Master* offers a module that will convert foreign currencies, as well.

Assess Health Insurance

Health insurance debates rage in Washington as I write this book. To be sure, the lack of a decent national plan is one of our deficiencies as a world power, but at least our elected officers are finally giving it some lip service.

A new software package called *Med$ure* serves as your health insurance manager. With *Med$ure* loaded on your computer, you can compare policies and options, print claim forms accepted by major insurers, coordinate benefits when two family members are covered by different plans, track claims from initial bill to final payment, flag outstanding claims, update children's growth and immunization records and chart genetic diseases in the Family Medical Tree. *Med$ure* author John Hawkins is the same guy who co-founded MECA software and persuaded Andrew Tobias to co-author *Managing Your Money*, by the way.

Go for It!

By now, you get the idea that there are plenty of financial organizers in the world of home software. Shareware catalogs, good BBSs, and on-line services like CompuServe and Prodigy can give you other good ideas on what's available in financial software. When you start taking advantage of your personal computer's organizational *élan*, you'll wonder how you ever managed without it.

Sources for
Personal and Household Finance Software

Checkbook Software
Andrew Tobias' Checkwrite Plus
($29.95, IBM-compatibles)
MECA Software, Inc., 355 Riverside Avenue
Westport, CT 06880, (800) 288-6322

CheckFree ($29.95, IBM-compatibles)
CheckFree Technologies, P.O. Box 897
Columbus, OH 43216, (800) 882-5280

Check Writer ($44.95, IBM-compatibles)
Dynacomp, Inc., 178 Phillips Road
Webster, NY 14580, (716) 265-4040

How to Handle a Checking Account
($49, Apple, IBM-compatibles)
Learning Seed Co., 330 Telser Road
Lake Zurich, IL 60047, (708) 540-8855

Financial Management Software

Andrew Tobias' Managing Your Money
($124.95, Macintosh, IBM-compatibles)
MECA Software, Inc., 355 Riverside Avenue
Westport, CT 06880, (800) 288-6322

Andrew Tobias' Financial Calculator
($29.95, IBM-compatibles)
MECA Software, Inc., 355 Riverside Avenue
Westport, CT 06880, (800) 288-6322

For the Record ($59.95, IBM-compatibles, Macintosh)
Nolo Press, 950 Parker Street
Berkeley, CA 94710, (415) 549-1976

MacMoney ($119.95, Macintosh)
Survivor Software, 11222 La Cienega Blvd., Suite 450
Inglewood, CA 90304, (310) 410-9527

Microsoft *Money* ($49.95)
Microsoft Corp., One Microsoft Way
Redmond, WA 98052-6399, (206) 635-7131

Money Counts ($35, IBM-compatibles)
Parsons Technology, 375 Collins Road NE
Cedar Rapids, IA 52402, (800) 223-6925

Quicken
($59.95, Apple, IBM-compatibles, Macintosh)
Intuit, 155 Linfield Avenue
Menlo Park, CA 94026-3014, (415) 322-0573

Retirement Analyzer
($25, IBM-compatibles, Macintosh)
Heizer Software, 1941 Oak Park Blvd., Suite 30
Pleasant Hill, CA 94523, (415) 943-7667

Will-Writing Sofrtware

It's Legal ($49.95, IBM-compatibles)
Parcons Technology, 375 Collins Road NE
Cedar Rapids, IA 52406-3120

Personal Law Firm ($99.95, IBM-compatibles)
BLOC Publishing, 800 Southwest 37th Avenue
Coral Gables, FL 33134, (800) 955-1888

WillBuilder ($59.95, IBM-compatibles)
Sybar Software, 2021 Challenger Drive, Suite 100
Alameda, CA 94501, (800) 227-2346

WillMaker ($69.95, IBM-compatibles, Macintosh)
Nolo's Living Trust ($79.95, Macintosh)
Nolo Press, 950 Parker Street
Berkeley, CA 94710
(800) 640-6656 (CA) (800) 992-6656, (415) 549-1976
Learn the real meaning of do-it-yourself and send for
their wonderful software/book catalog!

WillPower ($49.95, IBM-compatibles)
Jacoby & Meyers, 1156 Avenue of the Americas
New York, NY 10036, (800) 233-3109

Credit Repair Software
The Credit Report Repair Kit ($39, IBM-compatibles)
North Atlantic Publishing, P.O. Box 768111
Roswell, GA 30076, (404) 973-6637

Tax Software
Andrew Tobias TaxCut ($90, IBM-compatibles)
MECA Software, Inc., 327 Riverside Avenue
Westport, CT 06880, (203) 222-9150

MacInTax,
MacInTax for Windows
($99.95, Macintosh, IBM-compatibles)
IF:X Personal Tax Analyst
($79, Macintosh, IBM-compatibles)
Softview, Inc., 1721 Pacific Ave., Suite 100
Oxnard, CA 93033, (800) 622-6829

TurboTax for Windows,
TurboTax Macintosh
($59.95, IBM-compatibles, Macintosh)
ChipSoft, Inc., 6330 Nancy Ridge Drive, Suite 103
San Diego, CA 92121-9529, (619) 453-8722

Personal Tax Preparer ($49, IBM-compatibles)
Parsons Technology, Inc., 375 Collins Road, NE
Cedar Rapids, IA 52406-3120, (800) 223-6925

Real Estate Software
Landlord
Available via popular shareware distribution

PropMan (Disk #1179, 1180, 1452; IBM-compatibles)
PC-SIG, 1030 East Duane Avenue, Suite D
Sunnyvale, CA 94086, (800) 245-6717 (USA), (408) 730-9291

Real Estate Investment Analysis ($295)
Property Management ($395) (Macintosh)
Real Data, 78 North Main Street
South Norwalk, CT 06854, (203) 255-2732

Real Estate Analyst
Available via popular shareware distribution

Loan Software

Auto Finance Analyzer
($9; IBM-compatibles, Macintosh)
Heizer Software, 1941 Oak Park Blvd., Suite 30
Pleasant Hill, CA 94523, (415) 943-7667

Financer Super ($49.95, IBM-compatibles)
Zephyr Services, 1900 Murray Avenue
Pittsburgh, PA 15217, (800) 533-6666, (412) 422-6600

Loan Analysis ($21.95, IBM-compatibles)
Dynacomp, Inc., 178 Phillips Road
Webster, NY 14580, (716) 265-4040

Loan Manager ($49.95, IBM-compatibles)
Lassen Software, Inc., P.O. Box 2319
Paradise, CA 95967-2319, (800) 338-2126, (916) 877-0512

Loan Payoff Analysis ($9, Macintosh)
Heizer Software, 1941 Oak Park Blvd., Suite 30
Pleasant Hill, CA 94523, (415) 943-7667

Banker's Secret Software Package
($39.95, IBM-compatibles)
Good Advice Press, P.O. Box 78
Elizaville, NY 12523, (800) 255-0899

Stock Market Software

Fundgraf ($100, IBM-compatibles)
Parsons Software, 1230 W. 6th Street, Dept. C
Loveland, CO 80537, (303) 669-3744

Fundwatch Plus
($29.95, IBM-compatibles)
Lifestyle Software Group, 63 Orange Street
Saint Augustine, FL 32084, (904) 825-0220

StockFolio ($29.95, IBM-compatibles)
Zephyr Services, 1900 Murray Avenue
Pittsburgh, PA 15208, (412) 422-6600

Business Expense Software
Expense Master ($69.95, IBM-compatibles)
Danart Corp., 76 Belvedere Street
San Rafael, CA 94901, (415) 461-9100

Health Insurance Software
Med$ure ($89.95, IBM-compatibles)
Time Solutions Inc., 45 Kellers Farm Road
Easton, CT 06612, (203) 459-0303

Chapter Three

Computerize Your Hobbies and Collections

Hobbies are all those things we do for fun. And people can think of the most unusual ways to spend their spare time. There was a guy who collected horse's kidney stones, for example (to his credit, he *was* a veterinarian). And what about the woman who assembled paintings from dryer lint, or the man who ate an entire train, locomotive first.

For most of us, however, hobbies fall into more mundane categories: collections—or creative, technical, or social pursuits.

Your home computer can increase the fun of hobbies like stamp collecting, restoring old cars, or creative writing. And you'll be compounding hobbies: computers and whatever else you're into!

Tasks for Hobby Software

■ Log Ham Radio Contacts

■ Design Sewing, Needlecraft and Weaving Projects

■ Catalogue Coin, Stamp and Other Collections

■ Organize and Label Photos and Slides

■ Compose and Edit Music

■ Enhance Creative Writing Skills

■ Research Genealogy

■ Create Club Newsletters & Track Club Memberships

Ham Radio Software

Before there were computer nerds or even home computers there were ham radio nerds. With terminology like "input imped-ances," "reactive frequency values" and—well, you get the idea—this hobby's so technical it makes modeming look like hopscotch.

Now old-tech and new can merge when you use your home computer for ham radio activities.

A number of shareware diskettes provide the ham radio enthusiast with many fun and useful programs. It seems like ham radio users write shareware programs when they're not cruising the airwaves.

Many ham radio enthusiasts enter contests to see how many other enthusiasts they can contact. To the persistent goes the prize!

An amateur radio contest-logging program called *KB0ZP Super Contest Log* helps the operator log all those contacts. You can print out the log in a suitable format and enter them for prizes.

KB0ZP Super Contest Log's main screen shows date and time, name of contest, station call sign, grand total number of contacts made by mode and band, elapsed time from last contact, and total accumulated score. Up to 4,000 contacts can be logged. The program even includes help screens showing usable frequencies by band, class of license, and section abbreviations. For those amateur radio operators on the go, the program features a "hurry-up timer" that can time each contact.

Other software of interest to the ham radio enthusiast includes *MiniMuf*, a MUF (Maximum Usable Frequency) calculator for the amateur radio operator; *Morse*, a Morse Code–learning program; *Bearings*, for radio amateurs or anyone needing the precise bearings or great circle directions from one location to another; and *PC-Ham*, a set of amateur radio database programs (BASIC and *dBASE II* are required for *PC-Ham*).

Sewing, Weaving and Needlecraft Software

The home computer's graphics capabilities are ideally suited to garment design. Whether your medium is cloth, yarn or embroidery floss, sewing and crafts software can help you map out your project in advance—before time-consuming mistakes occur.

Sewing Software

Andros SoftWear's *SewSoft* line of Macintosh pattern-making software will change the way you live. And Andros president/programmer David J. Hall wouldn't have it any other way.

Hall has developed programs that print clothing patterns based on your body measurements. *SewSoft Bodice*, *Skirts* and *Pants* simplify ready-made pattern fitting by eliminating it altogether. The patterns, all basic shapes, can make up clothes for men or women. Dart lines and other detailing are printed right on the basic pattern; now you can become your own high fashion designer. Claude Montana, look out!

SewSoft makes sewing fun again, especially if you're not the mythical size 8 on the pattern envelope. (I, for one, will never have to shorten another waist or lengthen another sleeve again.)

On a deeper level, programmer Hall, who also teaches Yoga and practices Deep Tissue Massage, feels that clothing programs us.

Hall advocates that men should be free to wear, well, whatever they want. In particular, skirts. And in the spirit of breaking with traditions that may bind men mentally and physically, as he puts it, Hall has taken his beliefs on the road and all the way to the Johnny Carson and Phil Donahue shows.

Indeed, "Scots Wear Skirts" is the name of the Mac icon for his *Skirts* program.

When I related Hall's position to the men with whom I work, most chortled, predictably. One, a most distinguished gentleman who'd spent many years in Asia, told me how men there, himself included, wore lengths of cloth wrapped around in various ways whenever possible, especially in the hottest months.

No matter what you may think of Hall's philosophy, you'll love his software. For a detailed walk-through, let's check out *SewSoft Bodice*. This software really makes it easy to create custom-fitted shirts and blouses. You can store measurements on disk and churn out patterns for the whole family with this productive program.

To tailor clothing, 10 personal body measurements can be altered. These measurements specify a basic bodice, sloper or master pattern, which is printed onto six or more pages of standard printer paper. These pages are joined to form a full-size, precise pattern from which garments can be cut and sewn.

The program can be modified to produce a new sloper whenever there is a significant weight loss or gain. So, there's no need to cut down on those creme eclairs—your clothes will always fit.

SewSoft Bodice accommodates any adult body size or shape

for blouses, tops, or shirts. It also facilitates the adjustment of commercial patterns to individual shapes, and can be used to modify styles and copy the design of a ready-made garment.

An illustrated users' manual in a comprehensive three-ring binder explains the measurement-taking system, and a variety of screen displays guide a user through the operation of the system. Extra measurement forms are also provided.

A *Windows* version for MS-DOS computers is in beta-test; Hall also plans to include other types of patterns.

Weaving Software

Weaving is basically the creation of a grid, using yarns and other materials instead of paper and pen. Weaving software runs the gamut from simple grid creation and viewing in a program like Compucrafts' *The Weaver*, to a high-end, professional-quality software program like *Design & Weave*, which provides tools and options to let you produce exquisite and complex fabrics.

The Weaver features a set of utility programs designed to let a user warp, tie-up and weave an original design for visual assessment in seconds. The user needs no prior weaving experience and even less computer experience. Best of all, hours of painstaking work with a pencil and graph paper are eliminated.

While viewing a pattern on screen, the user can push individual treadles, erase individual wefts, stop a drawdown mid-screen, advance a row pointer, magnify the weave, and much more. The program is only available on the Apple series of computers, but the price of a used Apple II is so reasonable, serious weavers who have other computer systems should consider buying an Apple just for the loom room.

The Weaver's price is a bit more reasonable than other weaving packages.

Design & Weave's features include viewing and revising finished patterns on screen; printing a copy of a pattern plus all the technical information necessary to weave it; automatically computing plain weaves, twills and satins; combining two designs into one for more complex structures; performing repeats, symmetries, and picking motions, and more.

You can combine this program with other tools. With a plotter you can print out colored designs. Hooked up to the right monitor, you can see 16.7 million shades. The program zooms in and out to four different thread sizes, creates drawdowns and patterns for any loom, interfaces with the AVL Compu-Dobby system, and more.

Needlecraft Software

Drawing up designs for needlepoint or embroidery can be messy and time-consuming. A wonderful program called *Stitch Grapher* lets you draw, edit, save, and print needlecraft creations. With the planning out of the way, you have more time for what *really* matters in life: Counted-Cross Stitching!

Although I happen to use it for the craft I most enjoy, the program is not limited to just counted-cross stitch. Needlepoint, bargello, latch hook and design knitting enthusiasts will find that *Stitch Grapher* opens up a world of creative possibilities. In fact, any design that's done on a regular grid can be done on your computer. This means you're not limited anymore to buying pre-printed patterns, kits or books; if you can dream it up, *Stitch Grapher* can print it out.

Three companion programs can be ordered: Border1, Alphabet1 and Motif1. It's nice to have something already designed in case your imagination soars above your drawing skills! Future plans include EGA/VGA color support.

Compucrafts makes a Macintosh version, *Stitch Crafts*, that produces beautiful, high-resolution printouts. It has great editing/update features plus a lot more, but one feature really impressed me: A "counter palette" feature helps you determine the number of counts between any two locations or the dimensions of a particular motif. Simply click the mouse at the beginning square, drag it to the end and voila! Your count is displayed. Whew! Never be interrupted in the middle of counting all those tiny grid squares again! Future plans include a full-color, 16 million color edition and *Windows* version that will run on IBM-compatibles.

If you knit, you know that charting curves and other tricky parts of your garment could be easier. *Mom's Knitting Computer Program* for the Apple can help. Templates for necklines, sleeves, collars, and more can be filled in, edited, and printed out. Now you can knit something more complex than scarves and socks for Christmas gifts.

Cuddle Quilts

If quilting's your thing, call Prodigy and meet some of the fantastic people involved in the Cuddle Quilts project. Witness for yourself the power of home computing:

In the summer of 1989, Jan Weber started a fabric exchange on Prodigy's Quilting forum. When you joined, you received a package of squares in the mail, took a few, then added that number of squares from your own collection and mailed it on. That made it easy for quilters to collect a variety of fabrics for projects like Charm quilts, where no two pieces of fabric are alike.

Soon, women all over the nation were swapping fabrics in the mail, and swapping friendship and camaraderie in the process.

In May 1990, Jan's oldest son Michael was hospitalized and diagnosed with AIDS. Through him, she became aware of the Coming Home Hospice in San Francisco, where young AIDS patients whose families had rejected them could spend their last few months. She got the idea to present the hospice with a quilt.

Jan asked her pals on Prodigy to send her 12-inch pieced blocks; she was overwhelmed with the response. Some women sent a few blocks; several sent finished quilts. Non-quilters pitched in too: The crocheters and knitters sent finished afghans.

After a marathon block-fitting and quilting session in her front room, Jan and her husband took more than 40 quilts and afghans to the hospice on their first trip.

Many more quilts have reached the hospice patients since that first delivery. The patients, who have only a few months left, are touched by the warm sentiments embedded in the snuggly quilts. After completing a block, the Prodigy members sign it with their name and city. Jan said that sometimes, toward the end, patients who are weakened and can't get around very well just sit and run their hands over the quilts, gazing at the lovingly-crafted blocks and marveling at the names of strangers who cared enough to help them feel wanted.

Throughout the whole process, the Prodigy members have shared their joys and sorrows, writing to Jan about their own relatives with AIDS or other illnesses. "Our group is truly an electronic back fence," said Jan.

Jan started hosting quilting "brag-offs" and quilting parties for nearby Prodigy members. Around the same time, unbeknownst to her, Prodigy members were conspiring to make a quilt for her son, Michael. The pattern, "A Hole in the Barn Door," had been distributed to some 35 members across the nation, along with some beige fabric to back the blocks. The conspirators communicated via Genie, a competing on-line service, just so Jan wouldn't see their messages. At one of the get-togethers at her Stockton home, her Prodigy pals presented Michael's quilt to her.

When he saw the quilt, Michael was proud of the Prodigy members, and prouder still of his mom and the openness and love with which she had led this project.

The project keeps evolving. Currently, there's a new block theme each month. Right now, it's February, and the theme is hearts. Members send in as many (or few) blocks as they wish. When completed, the theme quilts will speak eloquently of the members' rich imaginations and skills. Above all, they will offer the recipients a touching reminder that someone cares.

If you aren't on Prodigy and would like to get involved, send a card to Jan and learn what the themes will be for the next few months. Or send any block; Jan will find a place for it. Jan Weber, 2527 South Jack Tone Rd., Stockton, CA 95215; (209) 463-3118. Jan welcomes donations of fabric and batting from companies and individuals, as well.

Collection-Traoking Software

Computers are perfect devices for keeping track of collections. The power of databases to search, sort and print data retrievals makes it a breeze to confirm the issue date of your obscure Guianan stamp. Spreadsheet features like automatic price updates let you keep an eye on the current market value of those priceless Spanish doubloons.

Collections aren't limited to stamps and coins, though. I once met a guy who collected vintage *TV Guides*. (He sold them for a pretty penny, too—especially the ones with Lucy on the cover.) The moral is, don't throw anything away, ever. And let your computer help keep it organized.

Specialized software tailored to stamp and coin collectors combines spreadsheet and database features and even offers simple text editors for word processor functions. If you don't collect stamps or coins, there are catch-all collection organizers available. If you don't find any software you can use, customize a simple database or spreadsheet program to your needs. In any case, collections are more enjoyable when you can see at a glance just what you've collected!

Collectibles DataBase is a great way to keep track of collectibles like figurines, plates, antiques and even home inventory. The package contains two programs: one for plates, and one for "just about everything else," according to program author Michael Belofsky.

For each piece in your collection, you can record details like series name, producer, purchase date and price, insured value and more. Add your own, user-defined rarity codes. You can sort by any category and print any report.

Michael also sells *Collectibles DataBase: Baseball (Sports) Cards & Comic Books*, a computer management system for paper collectibles. Now, a way to track those *TV Guides*!

COINS/PLUS is a coin inventory program that contains the descriptions and latest market-value information on more than 2,300 U.S. coins. Using convenient standard coin numbers, the program provides written records for investment, tax, insurance, and estate planning purposes, and tracks the value of your investment, automatically updating prices each year.

Comprehensive reports include: Value Report, which lists coins in a user's collection, what you paid for each coin, current value and resulting profit or loss to date; Collection Summary report, which provides bottom-line figures like total number of coins in a collection, total amount paid for them, and total present value; Coins Sold Report, detailing cost and profit figures on coins you've sold; and Want List, a buyer's guide in which you can indicate the coins needed to complete your collection.

The IBM-compatible shareware program *Coin File* keeps an inventory of coins and a want list and will print out an inventory sheet as well as mini labels for your coins.

The publisher of *COINS/PLUS* put out two sister programs that operate similarly, but are designed for stamp collectors. *STAMPS WORLD* helps inventory and evaluate your international or topical stamp collection, while *STAMPS* keeps track of all your U.S. stamps. Both programs generate extensive reports like those from *COINS/PLUS*, as well.

Commodore and IBM-compatible computer owners can get organized with *Collector's Paradise*, which contains inventory programs for coin collections, stamp collections, and rare collectibles. Another catch-all collection organizer is *The Collector*.

Photography Software

Most of you have all your photos neatly tucked into well-captioned photo albums, lined up in tidy rows on your bookshelves, right? Well, if you throw those carefully composed photos in the nearest shoebox the minute you get home from that vacation or family reunion (as I do), you can benefit from photography software. Organize those pictures (with the help of your computer) so they can be seen, enjoyed and reprinted for relatives and friends.

Most photo software offers the same basic features. There's usually a database and a labeling feature, keeping your voice from going hoarse after explaining all 12 rolls of vacation film. Your friends can simply read the label on the back of the picture, instead. To choose photo software, determine what type of program will best suit your needs. Some programs are designed for commercial photographers, while others are better suited to home uses.

Glacier Software's *Pic Trak* is a photo, slide, and album cataloguing system designed for people who want to organize business and personal photos for easy showing. This program is easy to get up and running and comes with free telephone support (although a long-distance call to Montana is required). The assortment of labels included runs from slide captions to labels for the backs of your photos.

STOCKvue is designed for the professional photographer. This program generates captions, catalogue entries, and submissions logs. The photographer who has trouble keeping track of when, where, and to whom photos were sent will appreciate this last feature. It dates submissions to tell you when photos are due back, noting when they are late. A menu selection even prints a customized form letter to remind a client of how many photographs are late and who received them. Data for each photograph tells you the photo's creator, film type, format, model releases, value, and earned income.

HindSight is a Mac program for the professional photographer. It does invoicing, tracking, follow-up letters, captions and more—and generates stylish Mac printouts every step of the way.

A shareware program for IBM-compatibles fills the needs of camera bugs for less money. *Photo Pack* is a collection of programs to help improve photo skills. There's a lens selection module, a darkroom timer program, a label maker, and a photo database.

Music Software

Composing and editing music on your computer is just as easy as composing and editing words on your computer. Hundreds of music software programs make exploring the world of sharps and trebles fun—and guarantee a measure of privacy for those who should be playing the radio, instead!

One of the most powerful composing tools available for both amateur and professional musicians, and those who just want to fool around, is *Cakewalk Professional*. This program turns your computer into a desktop-based professional music publishing studio. Complete input, editing, and notation tools help with quick compositions. Music is entered, edited and reviewed in a Score Window. Music may be entered into the program from the built-in library, or notes may be arranged on the staff by selecting them from the Note Palette or by playing them with the mouse via the program's piano keyboard. Lots of cut and paste options make editing a breeze.

One of *Cakewalk*'s more advanced features is a voice editor, which lets you create and modify your own warblings and add them to your compositions. Fun stuff! Once you've got it down,

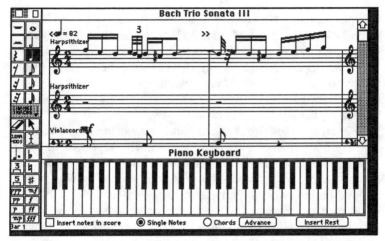

It's fun and easy to create and play music with a number of music programs

you can see what's going on in three ways: a measure counter, flashing notes and a player piano. Other advanced features include creating staccato, smooth, and vibrato sound effects; the ability to change parameters like key and time signatures, staffs and clefs, working space and score width; and the option of repeating scores and passages without actually replaying the piece. *Cakewalk* also features a keyboard recording function that copies everything you play, saving it until you're ready to play it back.

Less expensive programs like *Trax* for the IBM and Mac do almost as much. This is a quick moving field and you might do well to consult a MIDI magazine or call a MIDI-oriented BBS to learn about the latest hot programs.

On the shareware front, several programs for IBM-compatible computers let you try before you buy. *Composer* lets you easily create and edit music. Several programs of this type can turn your PC into a piano. Unfortunately, the PC only plays one note at a time, so you can't play chords, but you can change the pitch and duration of your notes. *Pianoman* is a bit more advanced, allowing cut and paste, search and replace.

Ibis Software makes two good music teaching programs: *Play It by Ear*, for ear training, and *Rhythm Ace*, for (you guessed it) rhythm training. *Ace* is compatible with Ad Lib or Sound Blaster sound cards. Got an IBM-compatible? If you do anything, add a sound card. They're getting more affordable and really enhance your gaming and music playing. Attach some inexpensive speakers to your computer while you're at it.

Creative Writing Software

Picture yourself, quill pen in hand, composing beautiful verse and exciting fiction. Now picture yourself, keyboard in hand, learning how to craft all that verse and fiction. The computer can tutor you in writing well, whether your writing hobby centers around fiction or poetry, script writing or sci-fi.

Writer's Workshop for the Macintosh offers writers and researchers the ability to organize freelance writing ideas, finances, and reference materials.

Three modules track financial records (for when you become good enough to get paid for your writing), ideas and submissions, and references. Searches and reports can be easily generated.

Six reference tools and a grammar checker come packed into one program for IBM-compatibles: *Writers Toolkit for Windows*. Whether it's common knowledge or a pithy quote, insert it into your deathless prose with the help of this powerful program.

In addition, hundreds of style and grammar checkers are available for every computer system. Mentioned before in the educational software section, *Readability* for IBM-compatible computers is one of the best writing aids around. Save an example of your writing as a text file, and bring it into *Readability*. Choose one of nine categories of writing you think it fits.

Categories range from "Children's books" to "Magazine feature articles" to "Bureaucratic gobbledygook." (I wonder if anybody ever chooses this last category.) You can see at a glance how your writing measures up in any of 16 diagrams. Suggestions for increasing your writing's readability follow. The hardcover manual is extensive and well researched.

Currently, *Readability* is available as shareware—a great deal at only $25. For an even more power-packed style program, try Scandinavian's commercial product: *Corporate Voice*. Pick any document written by any writer: *Corporate Voice* will tailor all future documents to that style. The possibilities are endless.

If poetry is your aim, WordPerfect Corporation makes *Rhymer*, a phonetic word finder. It lets you search 93,000 words phonetically using symbols that match any single sound, a vowel sound, and more. You can save your findings to disk, limit the scope of word searches and a lot more.

Script writers who use IBM-compatibles should try *Super-Script*, an authorized add-on to the popular *WordPerfect* word processor. This program sticks in all the complex formatting your script will need to pass through the studio gates on its way to fame and making you a fortune.

Genealogy Software

Genealogy is a popular hobby, judging by the number and scope of available genealogy software. Computer database and report-generating capabilities are natural helpmates to the detailed records necessary for genealogists. Computer graphics capabilities let you make neat coats of arms and other genealogy-oriented art and awards.

The two top-selling genealogy programs for the PC are *Roots III* and *Personal Ancestral File*. Both programs let you create reports and charts based on names, locations, and years. You can even publish formal family histories. *Roots III* can chart up to six generations per page, and the program automatically numbers and references continuation pages. Ancestor charts and family-group sheets let you easily calculate blood relationships between any two subjects. The manual weighs in at over 750 pages, answering all the genealogy questions you could ever dream up.

On the Macintosh front, *MacGene* lets you annotate individual records with baptism, occupation, military service details, and more. You can link records for fast access to charts, lists, and sorts. *Family Heritage File* can produce approved submission forms for all Latter-day Saints ordinances, as well as lists of individuals whose ordinance work has not yet been completed. *Family Roots* allows direct insertion of word processor files, letting you tell all the family secrets in as much detail as you want.

Horizons is an inexpensive IBM-compatible genealogy package that's designed expressly for the layman. It's simple yet comprehensive. One feature I liked was its ability to shoot off address labels. Family meetings and mailings are much facilitated, another example of PCs bringing joy to the homefront!

Shareware programs for IBM-compatibles let you try out the hobby and see if it's for you. *Family Ties* and *Family History* offer all the database capabilities the beginner is likely to need.

On Track

Keeping track of club and group members can turn a hobby into a full-time job! A shareware program for IBM-compatible computers can serve as a membership database for any group, club, or church. *Church Membership System* tracks members' birthdays and anniversaries, as well as other important dates. Special features include modify/delete, browsing, and multiple reports.

A program called *Who*, *What*, *When* helps manage group members, projects, and more. This is another program taken from the "productivity" software category, but it's ideally suited to keeping track of a busy club or social group. Meetings, people, and projects can be logged, and reports generated. A binder allows you to have a "hardcopy" of plans on hand anytime.

Prized Members

Awards and prizes are natural parts of club and hobby group doings. *Award Maker Plus* and similar programs let you print professional quality awards, certificates, licenses, coupons or anything you want. A new version, *Laser Award Maker*, brings the sharpness of laser output to your awards. Many of these programs include hundreds of pre-designed templates. Menu selection makes using them easy and fun. Call for a catalog of specialty parchments, frames, foil stickers seals and more.

Sources for Hobby Software

Ham Radio Software
Super Contest Log (Disk #1096)
Morse (Disk #939)
PC-Ham (Disk #562) (IBM-compatibles)
PC-SIG, 1030 East Duane Avenue, Suite D
Sunnyvale, CA 94086, (800) 245-6717 (USA), (408) 730-9291

Bearings ($24.95, Apple)
Zephyr Services, 1900 Murray Avenue
Pittsburgh, PA 15217, (412) 422-6600, (800) 533-6666

Sewing Software
SewSoft Bodice, Pants, or *Skirts*
($79.95 each; IBM-compatibles under *Windows*; Macintosh)
Andros SoftWear, 434 State Street
San Mateo, CA 94401, (415) 340-1040

Weaving Software
Design & Weave
($300, Macintosh)
AVL Looms, 601 Orange Street
Chico, CA 95928, (916) 893-4915, (800) 626-9615

The Weaver ($49.95, Apple)
Compucrafts, P.O. Box 326
Lincoln Center, MA 01773, (508) 263-8007

NeedleCrafts Software
Stitch Grapher
($89.95, Apple, IBM-compatibles)
Stitch Crafts
($150, Macintosh; *Windows* version planned for near future)
Compucrafts, P.O. Box 326
Lincoln Center, MA 01773, (508) 263-8007

Stitchmaster ($19.95, IBM-compatibles)
Personal Artworks, P.O. Box 8402
Kentwook, MI 49518

Knitting Software
Mom's Knitting Computer Program
($49.99, IBM-compatibles)
Triple-D Software, 823 N. 1340 East
Layton, UT 84041, (801) 547-9328

Collection Tracking Software
Collectibles DataBase
Collectibles DataBase: Baseball (Sports) Cards & Comic Books
($39.95, IBM-compatibles)
MSdataBase Solutions, 4635 Oak Creek Drive
Fort Wayne, IN 46835, (219) 486-6152

COINS/PLUS ($75; $30 each additional module;
IBM-compatibles, Macintosh, Apple)
Compu-Quote, 6914 Berquist Avenue
Canoga Park, CA 91307, (818) 348-3662, (800) 782-6775

Coin File (IBM-compatibles)
Pan World International, 422 Halsey Road
N. Brunswick, NJ 08902, (908) 821-6164

Stamps World ($32.50, Apple, IBM-compatibles, Macintosh)
Compu-Quote, 6914 Berquist Avenue
Canoga Park, CA 91307, (818) 348-3662, (800) 782-6775

Collector's Paradise
($39.95, IBM-compatibles; $29.95, Commodore 64/128)
Coindata ($49.95, IBM-compatibles)
Dynacomp, Inc., 178 Phillips Road
Webster, NY 14580, (716) 265-4040

Stamp Collector ($49, Apple, IBM-compatibles)
Coin Collector Catalog ($49, Apple, IBM-compatibles)
Andent, Inc., 1000 North Avenue
Waukegan, IL 60085, (708) 223-5077

The Collector ($85, IBM-compatibles)
The Third Rail, 3377 Cimmaron Drive
Santa Ynez, CA 93460, (805) 688-7370

Photography Software
Pic Trak ($89, IBM-compatibles)
Glacier Software, P.O. Box 3358
Missoula, MT 59806, (406) 251-5870, (800) 234-5026

STOCKvue ($300, Macintosh)
HindSight, P.O. Box 11608
Denver, CO 80211, (303) 791-3770

For Photographers (Disk #1164)
Photo Pack (Disk #1249) (IBM-compatibles)
PC-SIG, 1030 East Duane Avenue, Suite D
Sunnyvale, CA 94086, (800) 245-6717 (USA), (408) 730-9291

Music Software

Cakewalk Professional ($249)
Romeo Music Cakewalk Series ($29.95)
(IBM-compatibles)
Twelve Tone Systems, P.O. Box 760
Watertown, MA 02272, (800) 234-1171, (617) 273-4437

SpJr
($69.95; $129 with SoundBlaster Sound Card)
(IBM-compatibles)
Voyetra Technologies, 333 Fifth Avenue
Pelham, NY 10803, (914) 738-4500

Trax
($99, IBM-compatibles, Macintosh)
Passport Designs, 625 Miramontes Street
Half Moon Bay, CA 94019, (415) 726-0280

Finale
Music Prose (Call for current pricing)
Coda Music Software, 1401 E. 79th Street
Bloomington, MN 55425, (612) 854-1288

Composer (Disk #794)
Pianoman (Disk #279) (IBM-compatibles)
PC-SIG, 1030 East Duane Avenue, Suite D
Sunnyvale, CA 94086, (800) 245-6717 (USA), (408) 730-9291

Creative Writing Software

Writer's Workshop ($99, IBM-compatibles)
Futuresoft System Designs, Inc., 160 Bleecker Street, Suite 5JW
New York, NY 10012, (504) 837-1554, (800) 327-8296

Readability ($25)
Corporate Voice ($249, IBM-compatibles)
Scandinavian PC Systems, Inc., Six Nelson Street
Rockville, MA 20850-2130, (301) 294-7450, (800) 4-US SPCS
(They'll be relocating to Louisiana in late '92)

WordPerfect Rhymer
($49, IBM-compatibles)
WordPerfect Corp.
1555 N. Technology Way
Orem, UT 84057, (801) 225-5000

SuperScript ($99, IBM-compatibles)
Inherit the Earth Technologies, 1800 S. Robertson Blvd.
Los Angeles, CA 90035, (213) 559-3814

Genealogy Software
Roots III ($250, IBM-compatibles)
Commsoft, 2257 Old Middlefield Way
Mountain View, CA 94043, (707) 838-4300

Personal Ancestral File ($35, IBM-compatibles)
Church of Jesus Christ of Latter-Day Saints
50 E. North Temple Street
Salt Lake City, UT 84150, (801) 531-2584

MacGene ($145, Macintosh)
Applied Ideas, Inc., P.O. Box 3225
Manhattan Beach, CA 90266, (310) 545-2996

Family Roots ($180, Macintosh)
Quinsept, Inc., P.O. Box 216
Lexington, MA 02173, (617) 641-2930

Horizons ($39.95)
Lifestyle Software Group, 63 Orange Street
Saint Augustine, FL 32084

Family Ties (Disk #465)
Family History (Disks #361, #632) (IBM-compatibles)
PC-SIG, 1030 East Duane Avenue, Suite D
Sunnyvale, CA 94086, (800) 245-6717 (USA), (408) 730-9291

Club/Social Group Software
Church Membership System (Disk #742)
PC-SIG, 1030 East Duane Avenue, Suite D
Sunnyvale, CA 94086, (408) 730-9291

Who, What, When ($295, IBM-compatibles)
Chronos Software, Inc., 1500 16th Street, Suite 100
San Francisco, CA 94103, (415) 626-4244

Award Maker Plus
($49.95, Amiga, Apple II series, IBM-compatibles, Macintosh)
($39.95, Atari ST, Commodore)
Laser Award Maker ($199, IBM-compatibles, Macintosh)
Baudville, 5380 52nd Street, SE
Grand Rapids, MI 49508, (616) 698-0888, (800) 728-0888

Chapter Four

A Computer in the Garden

A computer in the garden? The image of mud-encrusted floppy disks comes to mind, but a computer can be as essential to the garden as a shovel or hose. Specialty gardening software programs have made America's favorite hobby easier and more enjoyable for beginners and "green thumbs" alike.

Gardening software integrates familiar computer processes like spreadsheets, databases, Gantt charts, and even word processors. All this functionality provides the gardener with one-stop organization and efficiency.

Today's gardening software helps the new gardener plot enough rows of corn to feed the family, or the landscaper select a compact shrub with bronze foliage and red blossoms. Whatever your gardening interests, a computer can maximize your gardening time and effort—leaving *you* more time to . . . smell the roses.

Tasks for Gardening Software

- Plant or Crop Selection
- Row/Plot and Landscape Planning
- Timing Plantings
- Scheduling Gardening Tasks
- Keeping Garden Records
- Printing Out Seed Orders
- Botanical Reference Guide

Plant or Crop Selection

One of the most difficult, yet enjoyable, gardening tasks involves neither rake nor shovel and seldom requires bending over.

That's deciding what to plant. We've all heard stories of the winter-bound gardener who can hardly wait for the seed catalogs to arrive in the mail. The fun part is pouring over the full-color plant descriptions, savoring each one and picturing your own garden overflowing with magnificent flowers and succulent vegetables. But most people have limited garden space, and narrowing down the plant wish-list is a cruel but necessary job.

After the usual method of going through the seed catalog and writing down every bush with blue flowers, then going back to pick out just those with dark-green foliage, and then narrowing down *that* list to just the drought-tolerant bushes, you'll probably give up and pour concrete instead. (Please don't give up that easily!) Load your computer with a plant database to make plant selection a snap.

Before your computer selects plants for your garden, the program asks where you live, when you'll be planting, and other particulars. You'll be asked some questions that help the computer customize the program for your region, garden size, preference for rows or beds, north/south or east/west orientation, and the like. Many programs ask for your zip code, so you don't accidentally choose a frost-needy fruit tree for a Southern California garden.

A set of programs from Infopoint Software, *Flower Finder, Bulb Finder* and *Plant Finder*, just about covers the gamut of growing things. Simply enter your desires and the programs list appropriate plants. You can browse through information on specific plants. Best of all, the programs let you change listings to reflect your specific experiences.

Data in these programs was obtained from an extensive horticultural library, as well as dozens of seed catalogs and many hours gabbing with master gardeners, according to Infopoint's Dorothy Nichols. Add to that list her many years of gardening experience.

Note: When you've answered the program's questions about your garden, you'll be asked to give that garden setup a name. The program will then save all your information to disk under that file name, giving you a record of the garden for posterity.

Selecting plants to meet a set of requirements is simply a matter of typing in your specifications under categories like bushes, blue-flowered, dark foliage or drought-resistant. The gardening software does a rapid search of its database, and displays a list of the plants fitting your criteria. Then type in each of the plants on this list, have the program do a search, and get ready to learn more about its cultural requirements.

Database sizes vary from program to program. So do the types of plants contained there. *Ortho's Computerized Gardening*'s database contains 750 ornamentals. *CHIP* (*Computerized Horticultural Information Planner*) offers several databases running under one program; each database averages 1,000 plant profiles in categories like Broadleaf Evergreens or Perennials. *Garden Manager* comes with 167 vegetables listed, with room for a total of 200.

Two other gardening programs also allow you to add your own favorites. *CompuGarden* lists 80 vegetables, herbs, and flowers, with room for 125 varieties. And *Gardener's Assistant* offers 55 vegetables; 45 more can be added. All of the programs allow modification of the database entries.

Row/Plot and Landscape Planning

Most people suspect that a plant's minimal light, food, and water requirements must be met in order for it to thrive. But there is a fourth factor to be considered: space. When deprived of sufficient room to grow, a plant is deprived of all those other requirements and suffers stress.

Stress can affect a plant in several ways, none of which will add to the beauty or bounty of your garden. Plant responses to stress range from poor growth, premature defoliation and scrawny flowers and fruits, to production of low-vitality seeds. Although questions of yield and fruit quality pertain mostly to the vegetable/fruit garden, ornamentals have space requirements too.

Gardening software lets you allocate every square inch of space, in advance, not by tearing out bushy growth after it's too late.

Once you've selected plants from the software's database, the program will ask how much you want to grow (or how many people you want to feed, in the case of vegetables). The program then goes to work, placing plants according to height, cultural requirements and tolerance for neighboring plants.

Several gardening programs will draw the layout on the screen, and you can print it out for later reference. (Much easier than lugging the monitor to your garden site.)

Landscape architects charge a tidy price. A program in Abracadata's home-CAD line, *Design Your Own Home: Landscape*, lets you arrange various shrubs and trees around your house, then ages them on screen to show you how the design will grow in.

Take the layout to the nursery and have a ball (a root-ball!) as you purchase computer-selected plants to enhance the value and beauty of your home.

A Blue-Ribbon Mac Program

It's rare to find Macintosh gardening software; surprising, since Macs are so great with graphics. Terrace Software's *Mum's the Word* (gardeners usually have great senses of humus!) runs on just about any Mac and offers a fully integrated gardening solution.

Combining object-oriented graphics with a database of horticultural information, *Mum's* unites garden design, info retrieval, plant selection and record keeping.

Lay out your garden with drawing tools that include a palette of shapes. Then search the database for the perfect candidate. Assign a plant to a shape in the layout, and *Mum's* automatically labels the area and adds the plant to a list of the layout's plantings.

Great feature: You can search the graphics as well as the text database! Simply double-click on a shape in your garden's layout and up pops all of the info for the plant you've assigned to that shape. Worried that a nearby shrub may shade a sun-loving annual? This feature lets you spot trouble in advance. And whenever a plant is added or deleted the list is automatically updated.

Mum's features an add-your-own database and comes with 300 entries, fully editable, to start you off. There's a space for notes on varieties, too. Programmer Roberta Norin is planning some great features in the upcoming upgrade, which should coincide with this book's release.

Gardening hats off to a well-thought-out program.

Timing Plantings

The worst thing a garden can have is patches of bare soil, unplanted, unloved. Besides being ugly, fallow corners promote weed growth and soil erosion. And you could be getting flowers or vegetables out of that space.

Gardening software enables you to take full advantage of what space you do have by planning when to start seedlings, transplant, thin within the rows, and harvest. Once you harvest, *CompuGarden* times up to four successive plantings—maximizing your garden's output. This program also offers another plus: it keeps track of each plant's location each year, automatically rotating that crop to another location the following year. Crop rotation is important. Even in a small garden it helps to curb disease and minimize the depletion of soil nutrients.

The beginning gardener can also benefit by learning what plants do better in what season. The database entry for eggplant indicates that, being a summer annual, spring sowing is advised.

Scheduling Gardening Tasks

Don't let your garden go just because you think it's more "natural." If left to its own devices, your garden will rule you and you'll rue your garden. Plants seem to go by their own timetable, and without a regular program of weeding, mulching, watering, planting, and seed starting, the garden can get out of hand quicker than you'd think. Even though you know what needs to be done, and intend to do it soon, you might forget or put off the task too long. In that case, why not let your computer keep you organized?

Gardening software uses the information you enter in the plant selection module to calculate your garden schedule. Based on the last frost date in your area, *Garden Manager* will indicate planting date, weeks for plant maturation, and weeks of harvest. You can view or print as many weeks as you wish. *CompuGarden* lets you view and print two types of planting schedules. A Gantt chart maps out the entire season's activities and shows when to start seeds in flats or beds, transplant, thin, fertilize, and harvest each crop. A weekly schedule summarizes tasks you need to accomplish each week. Both programs let you individualize the tasks.

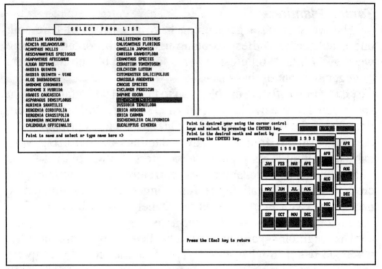

Garden schedulers make you stick to a plan, and your garden will love you for it.

Keeping Garden Records

Remembering the outstanding plant varieties of gardens past is easy. Every gardener can rattle off the name of the rose that produced dozens of blooms or the one cucumber that never succumbed to mildew. But who remembers the failures?

With the aid of gardening software, the computer can help you record all the varieties you try, good and not so good, so you don't get stuck with a mediocre variety again. You can then use this record to modify and personalize the plant database in future years.

Journal modules allow you to record data about the weather or unusual insect activity during a particular season, as well. Or anything else you feel is important. The journal module in *CompuGarden* has a separate productivity log area, where you assign a market value to each of the crops you grow. The program will then calculate the net value of your season's effort, subtracting labor, materials, and any other costs incurred. (Many gardeners won't want to use this feature!)

Gardening software allows you to print the various schedules, plant selections, garden plans, and database entries included in the program. Computers excel at generating records. Carry a printout out to the garden and see for yourself where the beans went two years ago.

Printing Seed Orders

You're taking a chance when you buy seeds at the local nursery or discount store. You rarely find a good selection, and you don't know how fresh the seeds are. Let your computer turn you into a mail-order gardener, instead!

Receiving garden catalogs in the mail is fun. And reading the descriptions and cultural notes is a great gardening education. What's more, they're almost always free.

The computer has helped you plan the garden and select your varieties, but now you have to go back and forth between your favorite seed catalogues and your variety printout to order your seeds. One program, *Garden Manager*, does away with the tedium involved in seed ordering.

While choosing your crops, *Garden Manager* lets you identify with a two-letter code what seed company carries what plant. You can then print separate variety lists sorted for each seed company, making the ordering process effortless. This list includes the number of plants you planned to grow, which helps in deciding how much seed of any one variety to buy.

Botanical Reference Guide

The database components of gardening programs are invaluable sources of information, particularly those programs offering larger databases. Sorting for different plant characteristics is easy with a computer. Most programs let you search by botanical and common names. But what if you forget a plant's name? *Ortho's Computerized Gardening* lets you use an asterisk to indicate that there are letters missing either before or after the typed letters. If you place an asterisk after a portion of a name, the selector chooses all the plants that begin with those letters. Conversely, you can place an asterisk before a portion of a name, and the plant selector will make a list containing plants with those letters anywhere in their names.

High and Low Points

For sheer number, *Hortis Opis* weighs in at 5,000 plants. Another plus: This PC and Mac plant database offers more variety than others, since it focuses on interesting, unusual plants. A new feature is the ability to export plant lists from *Hortis Opis* to your own word processing program. The future may hold a Mac version, as well, according to a J. Mendoza software spokesman.

On the minus side, *Ortho's Computerized Gardening* doesn't take full advantage of the computer's power. The landscape planner is a large piece of glossy grid paper, and a plant shopping list also comes on (ugh!) hardcopy. The plant selector database leaves out vegetables, so a vegetable planting guide is included—in the form of a poster. You can't add plants to the database, or modify existing listings. And if you need instructions on feeding requirements, spacing, pest susceptibilities, or how deep to plant, you'll have to consult the 192-page Ortho *Gardening Techniques* book tucked into the package.

The program is primarily a plant database—and an excellent one. In fact, this would make a great software addition for anyone interested in landscaping. The notepad and calculator (the latter accessible from anywhere in the program) are thoughtful additions.

Even though *Gardener's Assistant*'s main strength is garden layout, it plots the garden in single rows, which is useless for people with small gardens or those who prefer beds. And if you choose too much of one vegetable for your garden size while selecting plants, *all* of your plant choices are wiped out—and you're zapped back to the main menu.

On the other hand, *CompuGarden* bases all its plantings on 4-foot wide raised beds. Even though raised beds are an excellent way to go, especially if you have clay soil, it would be nice to have a choice in the matter. Every garden (and gardener) is different. In light of *CompuGarden*'s all-around superiority in this software category, however, this is a small drawback.

Alternatives to Gardening Software

You can put your computer to work in your garden even if you don't own any specialty gardening software. Conventional word processors, spreadsheets, and databases can be used to keep journals, plot plots, and count costs. Those of us who can't live without the latest seed catalogs can even print address labels.

Got a modem? Join one of the national on-line services. CompuServe offers The Good Earth special interest group, where a gardening forum allows members to exchange tips and questions as well as gardening programs (shareware and member-written, of course). CompuServe recently went to monthly rates for general forums, so it's now a bit more affordable for the average gardener (who'd rather spend money on plants than on connect-time).

Prodigy members, too, head for an extensive gardening area on the Homelife Bulletin Board. Stumped? (No pun intended!) You can address questions to the Victory Garden experts, who hail from the Public Television program of the same name. Knowledgeable amateurs are quite willing to spout advice, as well. Last time I logged on, members were excited about an herb special-interest group they were forming. Lore on basil and dill was flying back and forth, and members were gearing up to start exchanging seeds through the U.S mail. Imagine: free seeds for the price of a stamp.

One of the joys in logging onto Prodigy's Garden area is seeing the automotive messages there. Apparently some users mistake "garden" for "garage," and type in urgent pleas for carburetor advice. And, sure enough, carburetor follows camellia in the list of current topics! The gardeners giggle, and try to restrain themselves from snide remarks. (They hardly ever succeed.) It's fun to guess whether the grease monkeys are goading the gardeners on purpose. . . .

Don't Let Your Computer Grow Moldy

If this chapter has succeeded in its aim, by now you're sitting at your computer, last year's seed packets in hand, jotting down notes about the best performers in your word processor. That's just a start. Send for one of these gardening programs, or find even newer and better ones on local software store shelves or bulletin board file lists, and watch getting organized become as fun as gardening itself.

Sources for Gardening Software

CHIP (database modules average $350; program costs $600;
call for availability of special "beta test-site" deal)
(IBM-compatibles, Macintosh)
Paradise Information Inc., P.O. Box 1701
East Hampton, NY 11937, (516) 324-2334, (800) 544-2721

CompuGarden
($69.95, IBM-compatibles)
CompuGarden, Inc., 1006 Highland Drive
Silver Spring, MD 20910, (301) 587-7995

Design Your Own Home: Landscape
($89.95, Apple, IBM-compatibles, Macintosh)
Abracadata Ltd., P.O. Box 2440
Eugene, OR 97402, (800) 451-4871

Flower ($89.95)
Bulb ($49.95)
Plant Finder ($89.95)
(Set of three for $99.95; IBM-compatibles)
InfoPoint Software, P.O. Box 83-3
Arcola, MO 65603, (417) 424-3424

The Gardener's Assistant
($25, IBM-compatibles)
Shannon Software, Ltd., P.O. Box 6126
Falls Church, VA 22046, (703) 573-9274

Garden Manager
($49.95, IBM-compatibles)
Jeff Ball and Gary Gack, P.O. Box 338
Springfield, PA 19064, (800) 527-8200

Hort-a-Sort ($79.95, IBM-compatibles)
Hortis Opis ($250, IBM-compatibles; Macintosh upcoming)
J. Mendoza Gardens, Inc., 18 East 16th Street
New York, NY 10003, (212) 989-4253

Landscape Plant Manager
($50, IBM-compatibles)
Ferris State College, Dept. of Bio Science
Big Rapids, MI 49037

Mum's the Word Plus ($165)
Mum's the Word ($125) (Macintosh)
Terrace Software, P.O. Box 271
Medford, MA 02155, (617) 396-0382

Ortho's Computerized Gardening
($49.95; IBM-compatibles; Apple II, Commodore, Mac Plus)
Ortho Information Services, 575 Market Street
San Francisco, CA 94105, (415) 894-0277

CompuServe Information Services
P.O. Box 202012, 500 Arlington Center Blvd.
Columbus, OH 43220, (800) 848-8199, (614) 457-8600

Prodigy Services
(800)-PRODIGY

Chapter Five

*Health and Nutrition on Your
Home Computer*

When asked to picture a computer user, you probably imagine a pale, unkempt, out-of-shape blob with a greenish smile and glazed eyes. All computer users are not the Purple People Eater! And a new breed of health-oriented computer software is dashing those old stereotypes to bits. After all, keeping healthy involves staying organized, and the computer is certainly fit in that area.

Diet and nutrition software packages contain extensive databases to help keep tabs on your food consumption for the day. The software makes use of your computer's math abilities to calculate total intake of calories, fats, vitamins, and other nutrients. If you're forced to say "diet," some programs include motivational essays to get you psyched up for a new physique.

Let cuisine software help you choose recipes with only the healthiest, in-season ingredients. Food preparation software makes keeping healthy a job you share with your computer.

(No fair punching in "cheesecake" as a primary ingredient, though.)

The culinary arts take on a new, high-tech appeal with the many cuisine packages on the market. You can even download recipes from Prodigy and CompuServe directly into some programs, and do away with retyping for good.

Never worry again about serving the proper beverage when your computer acts as your wine steward and bartender. Selecting just the perfect drink is fun when you put the proper software to work. And you'll find that Chardonnay goes with so many more things than Jolt Cola ever did.

Although it's no substitute for a doctor, your computer, loaded with stress-monitoring software, can help you head off any poor health habits. Exercise is a perfect stress reducer, and the right software can keep track of those laps swum, or miles jogged or biked, too.

Tasks for Health and Nutrition Software

■ Monitor Your Diet and Calorie Intake

■ Create Gourmet Specialties

■ Choose Appropriate Wines and Cocktails

■ Keep an Eye on Stress and Poor Health Habits

■ Diagnose Simple Health Disorders

■ Organize Your Exercise Schedule/Track Your Workouts

Diet and Nutrition Software

Typical of programs in this category is one for the IBM-compatible family of computers called *Munch*. *Munch* asks you to input all the foods you eat throughout the day. The program then analyzes their caloric and nutritive values, based on the Exchange System. Developed by the American Diabetes Association, the Exchange System divides foods into six basic lists or exchanges: milk, vegetable, fruit, bread/starches, meat, and fat. Within each group, the foods contain roughly equal amounts of protein, carbohydrates, fat, and calories—thus you can *exchange* one for another.

Munch's main menu lists 12 exchanges. The other six exchanges result from the program dividing the meat/dairy exchange into low, medium, and high fat groups. Additional categories come from fun-, combination-, and free-food exchanges.

Say you choose an exchange like milk. *Munch* asks you to enter the number of 1-cup servings of milk, yogurt, or sour cream you've consumed that day. Although the manual advertises the program's ability to accept fractional amounts, this pertains only to amounts over the one-serving minimum—so I didn't enter the $\frac{1}{4}$ cup of milk I add to my morning coffee. Another drawback is trying to mentally note your servings of each exchange member until you've scanned the entire list and entered the total. It would be easier to flag each food as you come to it and have the program keep a running total.

At the end of each exchange, the screen tells you how many grams of nutrients and calories have gone down your gullet. You get a similar report after entering all the day's exchanges, along with a short recommendation for balancing your intake. After spitting out a 1135 calorie total composed of 17 percent Fun Foods, one day's report admonished me: "Small percentage or nothing from this group usually results in better nutritional intake." Sadly, there's no way nerds can adjust this module.

That daily report can be printed or saved by labeling with a date. A history printout averages all the saved reports. *Munch*'s reports are a bit on the sparse side, however. I was told that my intake of 1135 calories for the day was 27 percent below the 1,557 calories a person of my age, dimensions, and activity level should consume. Yet nowhere was listed a goal to which a person of my build could aspire.

Another program, *Food Processor II*, lets you enter the specifics for your current weight or for your goal weight, giving you a better idea about how to reach that goal. This program goes into detail on vitamins, trace minerals and the like, and includes an extensive reference book.

Whatever the drawbacks, this program and others like it force you to examine and record your intake. This leads to guilt and self-loathing, feelings that can either help or hinder dieting.

On the shareware front, *MealMate* lets you enter a given food, a whole recipe, or an entire meal. After a run through its huge database, it spits out the nutritional lowdown. The program contains such scale-tippers as Camembert cheese and angel food cake. But those with truly gourmand tendencies can use the append feature to add favorites that *MealMate*'s programmers missed.

If all this database measuring forces you to take some measures of your own, a shareware program for IBM-compatibles called *Managing Your Food* lets you plan your shopping list according to nutritional values *and* cost.

Diet Pro for Windows contains every feature you'd ever want, including color charts that let you see how you're doing. It analyses 5,000 foods in all, and tracks 36 nutrients. A neat feature lets you plug in your exercise or fitness program. It even helps you develop an exercise plan, and suggests workouts! *Diet Pro for Windows* opens a window into the benefits of exercise: it provides a list of activities sorted by energy expenditure or alphabetically. You can add, change or delete exercises. You enter recipes and analyze them.

We all know exercise is the only real way to get into shape—combined with small portions of healthy food, of course. This program features graphic screens that make it easy to see imbalances in your nutritive intake.

East Meets West Nutrition Planner, from Japanese-specialty publisher Ishi Press, asks you to record every meal you eat for a year. The program lets you save an oft-repeated meal under a label, such as "Egg Breakfast," allowing you to plug in the meal as a whole, rather than as separate food entries.

Santé combines the best of diet and recipe software, including 415 dietician-tested recipes. It has a 3,000-food database, and "quietly" reminds you of your progress. It outputs colorful charts that quickly explain why last summer's bathing suit doesn't look quite as "oommpff" as it should.

Cuisine Preparation Software

"What's for grub?" The familiar refrain greets you every evening, no matter how harried or hassled your day's been. Unfortunately, the answer often may be less than inspired. Why not let the computer help plan and execute meals? The many cuisine preparation software packages available provide new ideas for familiar ingredients or can suggest new foods with which to experiment.

If you enjoy browsing through good cookbooks, cuisine software's searching abilities can let you explore particular foods or methods in depth. *Great Chefs of PBS*, for most computer systems, even includes biographies on famous chefs.

If everybody considers *you* a world-class chef, you'll find recipe programs that let you file, sort, and retrieve your own indispensable masterpieces. And many of the cuisine disks allow you to add your own creations.

The folks on Prodigy's Food and Wine Bulletin Board are all excited about one shareware program in particular, called *Meal Master*. Maybe that's because they can swap recipes directly using the service. Beginning with *Meal Master* release 6.20, a special export format is available.

Using this format, and a shareware utility named Pro-Util, users can upload recipes directly to Prodigy for other users. They can also download recipes that others have posted, and import them directly into *Meal Master* without any retyping. For more information on Pro-Util contact the author, Pete Royston, Prodigy ID DBRK81A. The procedures for exchanging recipes this way can be discussed on-line in the Prodigy "Food and Wine" forum. Jump "Food and Wine," select "Bulletin Board," then select the "Food Forum" topic.

Speaking of Prodigy, there's enough material to go through on its food forums to ensure you don't have time to cook! Various experts give advice, and there's always a plaintive request for some long-lost recipe. Fun stuff!

The computer's organizational abilities can help you revitalize family dinners, but why not enlist its help in planning a surprise dinner party? The ability to flag various dishes as you browse, then save them to a dinner menu file, is one of *Micro Kitchen Companion*'s best features.

Would you like to re-create the meal you made that special night for that special someone? Punch in the file name you saved, and voilà, it's ready to help you relive your memories. Conversely, avoid serving the same meal to the same guests by searching for their names in your Notes field.

Cuisine software often offers modules to assist in shopping as well as chopping. Most of the *Micro Kitchen Companion* software will re-size recipes for up to 999 guests—which does away with risky and tedious recipe multiplication tasks. This program interfaces with the *Great Chefs of PBS* series, too.

If the smell of bread baking in the oven is too much to resist, a shareware offering for IBM-compatibles can offer mouth-water ing, fragrant creations in an instant. *Computer Baker* lets you choose between 99 recipes from six categories: snacks, fudge and candy, muffins and biscuits, cookies, cakes and frostings, and pies. The documentation even defines the word "homemade" as "made from scratch" (for those who have been sitting in front of a computer a little too long).

Wine and Cocktail Selection Software

Although it's not as good a listener as Joe the bartender down at the neighborhood pub, your computer will never kick you out at 2 a.m. Programs specializing in mixology (bartending to you and me) let you wow your friends and sample new and exotic drinks at the press of a key. A plus with most bartending programs is that they let you search by liquor type. If you have too much of that slim-price vodka sitting around, your computer can search for ways to use it up.

Another electronic barkeep, *Mr. Boston's Official Micro Bartender's Guide Deluxe*, runs on every type of computer. This classic, converted to disk, contains a staggering 1,000 recipes, plus a listing of wine and beer selections. A VIP party-planning module lets you pick the drinks your guests enjoy most, and will even prepare a shopping list right down to the correct glassware. You can re-size recipes for up to 999 guests (but you'd better have a huge punchbowl). Search on fields like ingredients, personal preference, season, mood and more!

The *Micro Wine Companion* series of programs is available for almost every computer operating system. These programs are fun to use and add a touch of high-tech savvy to any meal. You can even pull up a chart of your cavernous wine cellar. Unsure of your selection? The program contains more than 300 reviews. Thousands of brands, labels, and vintners are included, so you'll never make a *faux pour* again.

Stress and Preventive Medicine Software

For information retrieving abilities, you can't beat a computer. A program called *Expert Express: Your Health* contains a knowledge base of 5,000 pages on dozens of health topics like stress, biofeedback, cancer and nutrition, AIDS, smoking and more.

Cholesterol is a common concern among health-conscious Americans. We have slowly come to realize that we can't shove fatty, nutrient-void foods down our throats forever without some kind of toll on our systems. Two programs for IBM-compatible computers help monitor cholesterol intake. Alternatives to killer foods are suggested in a non-nagging way.

```
 F1-Help| F2-Tools | Shift_F1-Detail Help |  The 8-Week Cholesterol Cure
    Daily Analysis ──────── Goal / Personality ────────
    Daily Summary
    Food Database    ight
    Secure Data              Male
    Print Manual     evel    Active
    Quit Program     er Day          <man 15 cal/lb><woman 12>
                     from Fat        <20-30% recommended>
          Cholesterol in mg/day      <100 mg/1000 cal>
```

```
┌ Day ─────────────────── Menu ───────────────────
│        Food         │ Units │ Measure │SFAT│MFAT│PFAT│WT G│CAL│FAT│CHOL
│                     │       │ Cup     │    │    │    │    │   │   │
│                     │       │ Cup     │    │    │    │    │   │   │
│                     │       │ Cup     │    │    │    │    │   │   │
│                     │       │ Cup     │    │    │    │    │   │   │
│                     │       │ Cup     │    │    │    │    │   │   │
│                     │       │ Cup     │    │    │    │    │   │   │
│ Total               │       │         │    │    │    │    │   │   │
```

Cholesterol tracking is effortless when your computer does all the work.

Take Control of Cholesterol, based on the bestseller *Eater's Choice* by Doctors Ron and Nancy Goor, offers a way to systematize your fight against cholesterol. After undergoing the program's questionnaire, the system determines your ideal intake of saturated fats. Using this information and your own dietary likes and dislikes, it helps you plan healthful menus using 200 recipes and 1,700 foods. It tracks your actual intake and helps find less lethal alternatives. A pop-up Dietary Ledger feature makes it easier to monitor your progress. A superior feature offered by *Take Charge of Your Cholesterol* is the on-screen running total of all the cholesterol and calories you've accumulated since the first day of your diet.

The 8-Week Cholesterol Cure is based on—and comes with—the well known bestseller of the same name. Charts from the book help you input the ideal number of calories you must consume and the cholesterol level you must maintain daily. The acid test comes after comparing your ideal daily cholesterol and caloric needs with your actual food intake. The Daily Analysis section is firm but kind, giving you better alternatives in case you're not meeting your goals.

Some foods just don't agree with us. Food allergies and sensitivities can be hard to pin down, however, because we usually combine many foods at mealtimes. Your computer is a perfect tool to help isolate those ingredients that aren't your cup of tea. *Well-Aware Food Sensitivity Software* helps you spot the foods to which you have allergies, then plans nutritious balanced menus with the foods that make you feel good.

An entire health database is offered by the *Expert Express: Your Health* software program for the IBM-compatible family of computers. The program provides instant access to a 500-page knowledge base of health information from the U.S. Government.

If you have children, or a hypochondriacal partner, a medical advisory software package might be handy to have around the house. These programs have you answer a series of questions, then progressively narrow down the possible maladies. *FamilyCare Software*, for IBM-compatible and Macintosh computers, is modeled upon the diagnostic process used by doctors to help parents with their childrens' medical problems. A shareware program, *Parents Home Companion: Managing Colic*, provides parents and those responsible for childcare with expert assistance in a range of common problems. An "artificial intelligence" scheme lets your answers guide you to new question banks.

On the more cerebral side, *Stress and Shrink*, a group of shareware programs, flags any dangerous mental imbalances you might be experiencing. One of the programs takes you through the Holmes Life Change Index, that infamous list of the 43 most stress-provoking life events.

Shrink, also shareware, asks you to list your preferences in many realms and then pigeonholes you neatly into one of four personality types. Another shareware offering called *Health Risk* evaluates your exposure to environmental and hereditary perils such as pollution, smoke, or lousy cooking.

A program called *PC-Relax* offers shapes and colors at which you can gaze in order to relieve stress and eye fatigue. *Vision Aerobics* offers dancing screens to either relax or stimulate your eyes, depending on what type of task you've just been doing.

Continuum is a game, or is it a meditative, relaxing tool? You can "play" in one of two modes. The competitive mode is frustrating, as you try to jump onto different shapes in a virtual reality-type universe. Relaxation mode can be a good time to focus on something besides immediate issues. The program offers you the chance to explore different moods. Background music matches the moods if you have a sound card.

Lifeguard, a terrific program, tells you when to take breaks to prevent computer strain. It asks you to program the intervals of work, and when it's time for a break, a sound-file tells you to "Cool It," in Bart Simpson's voice, or dozens of other ways. It suggests exercises you can do at your desk, for eyes, shoulders, back, and more.

Synchronicity offers you a moment of soothing sounds and meditative messages before you get back into the grind. It uses soft methods to find a way out of your problems.

The sounds of running water and frogs at boot-up signal that this is no ordinary computer program. *Synchronicity* greets you by name or calls you "friend," and asks you to relax your neck and shoulders before you type what's bothering you. You're urged to let go of thinking for a moment; to breathe and let go of your expectations. "Desire to know only what is true," says the full moon on screen. After picking up a few keywords from your earlier entry, you're invited to sit beside a stream and gaze upon a lantern, and beyond to a full moon with wispy clouds. Again, a stream gurgles and frog ribbits fill the air, taking you far from work or troubles and helping you to "center."

Once you've focused on your question for a few minutes, the program asks you to take some deep breaths and tap three times on your keyboard. Your keywords spin before you, faster and faster around the lantern's flame until they disperse into the air. Then you see a reading from the I-Ching, "The Book of Changes," an ancient Chinese book of wisdom.

Readings range from bending like a willow to triumphing through discipline. The program's charm lies in its ability to juxtapose your "real-time" problem with these ancient—and random—maxims. New insights can crowd your mind after watching *Synchronicity* combine ideas. Or, you may reject the pairings as meaningless to your situation, and start anew.

Either way, you've enjoyed a relaxing interlude and prepared for a calm, untroubled solution to come to you.

Sometimes you feel edgier than a hungry zoo jaguar with only a wire cage standing between him and a stroller-straddling toddler.

And you don't know why. Well, anxiety is a disabling force. But tension, anxiety's near cousin, can be a creative tool.

What's the difference between anxiety and tension? It's focus. If you feel anxiety, chances are you don't know exactly what's eating you. Tension, on the other hand, generally stems from some specific irritant.

Have you ever heard the phrase, "Creative tension"? It's true: If nothing ever opposed us, we'd linger forever in a state of self-satisfied stagnation. Well, identifying the source of tension is the first step to creatively acting on it. And two very different software programs can help.

If you want to learn how seemingly independent events affect your life, try using *The Emotional Spreadsheet*. Behind the oxymoronic name lies a system designed by a therapist to find correlations in a person's behavior patterns. Being aware of these patterns lets you make constructive, focused changes—to create the kind of life you want.

Simply enter questions on which you want data collected. You can either choose the sample question template or design one of your own. Tell the program if you'll be entering answers on a daily, weekly, or more infrequent basis, then save your questionnaire with a name. You can even "lock" it with a password—ensuring that your quest for self-knowledge remains private.

Although each questionnaire can hold 100 questions in 16 categories, *The Emotional Spreadsheet*'s notebook-like manual recommends you pare it down to no more than 25 questions, something you can work through in about 10 minutes. This keeps both the answering and analyzing process a pleasure, not a chore.

What types of questions will be important to you? There's no telling: Sample questions in the manual serve as invaluable guidelines, and you can alter your emotional spreadsheet as much as you want. Simply adding a question like "How much time did I spend on the phone?" to your spreadsheet's At Work category can help you see where all your time goes, and perhaps give you insight into that "I don't get anything done at work" anxiety. Seeing relationships between questions on exercise, alcohol consumption and daily stress levels may help you get a handle on that bout of insomnia you've had lately. And totaling the hours you spend with a parent, child, or pet may help you to do something positive to relieve guilt feelings that may be bothering you.

This program doesn't have to center around your mental states, however. With analytical tools like graphs, statistical counts, and keywords, you could apply *The Emotional Spreadsheet* to surveys, trend analysis, or other business matters.

Drawbacks: there's no Mac version yet, and you can't cut and paste questions from different spreadsheet files. These are minor flaws in such a revolutionary program. Why not try it and see if any new answers come to light?

For relaxation, try a public domain fractal program, especially if you have an IBM-compatible system equipped with an EGA/VGA monitor? You'll be reminded of the light show–saturated concerts of the late '60s (or perhaps a paisley necktie, depending on your age). The better your monitor, the more fun you'll have. Some fractal programs even come with sound.

Exercise Monitoring Software

Electronic devices for monitoring your workouts are common. Why buy yet another clumsy, expensive gadget when you already own a perfect tool for the job? Computer software can make sure you're getting an optimum workout, whatever way you choose to sweat.

The Athlete's Diary logs workouts, breaking commands down into easy, single keystrokes. Search on several fields to come up with your own Personal Best.

Running Counts has a feature called a Shoetrack System, which tracks the number of miles a pair of shoes has covered. Worn-out shoes are behind many accidents and injuries, so as fanciful as this feature sounds, it's important.

Runners will appreciate *Graphic Coach*'s ability to display each run graphically. The program calculates the pace for each training and racing day. It can present all your runs in monthly or yearly tables and can calculate and display a specific training schedule for the next week based on your most recent 5K or 10K race elapsed time. The schedule, based on calculated aerobic capacities, maximizes your training effort.

Sources for Health and Nutrition Software

Diet and Nutrition Software

DietPro for Windows
($59.95, IBM-compatibles running *Windows* 3.0 or higher)
Lifestyle Software Group, 63 Orange Street
Saint Augustine, FL 32084, (800) 289-1157, (904) 825-0220

The Diet Balancer ($59.95)
Nutridata Software, P.O. Box 769, 223 Meyers Corners
Wappingers Falls, NY 12590, (800) 922-2988

East Meets West Nutrition Planner
($49.95, IBM-compatibles)
Ishi Press International, 1400 N. Shoreline Blvd., Suite A7
Mountain View, CA 94043, (408) 944-9900

Fast Food Micro-Guide ($59, Apple)
Learning Seed Co., 330 Telser Road
Lake Zurich, IL 60047, (708) 540-8855

Food Processor II
($295–$395; Apple, IBM-compatibles, Macintosh)
ESHA Research, P.O. Box 13028
Salem, OR 97309, (503) 585-6242

MacNutriplan ($75, Macintosh)
MicroMedx Software Corp., 187 Gardiners Avenue
Levittoun, NY 11756, (800) 535-3438

Managing Your Food (Disk #1056; IBM-compatibles)
PC-SIG, 1030 East Duane Avenue, Suite D
Sunnyvale, CA 94086, (800) 245-6717 (USA), (408) 730-9291

MealMate (Disk #700; IBM-compatibles)
PC-SIG, 1030 East Duane Avenue, Suite D
Sunnyvale, CA 94086, (800) 245-6717 (USA), (408) 730-9291

Munch ($39.95, IBM-compatibles)
C.R. Smolin, 7760 Fay Avenue, Suite J
La Jolla, CA 92037, (619) 454-3404

Nutritionist II ($295, IBM, Macintosh)
Nutritionist III ($495, Apple)

N-Squared Computing, 5318 Forest Ridge Road
Silverton, OR 97381, (503) 364-9270

Nutri-fax ($59.95, Amiga)
Meggido Enterprises, P.O. Box 3020-191-A02
Riverside, CA 92159, (714) 683-5666

Santé ($59.95, IBM-compatibles)
Hopkins Technology, 421 Hazel Lane
Hopkins MN 55343-7116, (612) 931-9376, (800) 397-9211

Cuisine Preparation Software
Micro Kitchen Companion ($49.95)
Great Chefs of PBS Series ($39.95)
(Apple, IBM-compatibles, Macintosh)
Lifestyle Software Group, 63 Orange Street
St. Augustine, FL 32084, (800) 289-1157 (904) 825-0220

Computer Baker (Disk #1171) (IBM-compatibles)
PC-SIG, 1030 East Duane Avenue, Suite D
Sunnyvale, CA 94086, (800) 245-6717 (USA), (408) 730-9291

Recipe-Fax ($44.95)
Desserts Cookbook ($14.95)
Variety Cookbook ($14.95, Commodore Amiga)
Meggido Enterprises, P.O. Box 3020-191
Riverside, CA 92519-3020

Chef's Accountant ($59.95, IBM-compatibles)
Online Search, P.O. Box 300247
Arlington, TX 76010, (817) 468-8465

Wine and Cocktail Selection Software
Mr. Boston's Official Micro Bartender's Guide ($29.95)
Micro Wine Companion ($49.95), *World of Wine* Series ($14.95)
(Apple, Atari, Commodore 64/128, IBM-compatibles, Macintosh)
Lifestyle Software Group, 63 Orange Street
St Augustine, FL 32084, (800) 289-1157(904) 825-0220

Stress and Preventive Medicine Software
Expert Express Your Health ($49.95, IBM-compatibles)
Professional Knowledge Systems Inc.,
Twenty South Central Avenue, P.O. Box 16614
Saint Louis, MO 63105-1114, (314) 721-1510, (800) 727-1510

Take Control of Cholesterol ($19.95, IBM-compatibles)
Lifestyle Software Group, 63 Orange Street
St. Augustine, FL 32084, (800) 289-1157(904) 825-0220

The 8-Week Cholesterol Cure
($39.95, IBM-compatibles)
Disk-Count Software, 1751 W. County Road B, #107
St. Paul, MN 55113, (612) 633-0730

Expert Express: Your Health ($49.95, IBM-compatibles)
Professional Knowledge Systems, Inc., P.O. Box 11683
St. Louis, MO 63105, (800) 727-1510

Family Medical Advisor ($39.95, IBM-compatibles)
Navic Software, 5606 PGA Blvd., Suite 211
Palm Beach Gardens, FL 33418, (407) 622-3715

Familycare Software
($59.95, IBM-compatibles, Macintosh)
Lundin Laboratories, Inc., 29451 Greenfield Road
Southfield, MI 48076, (800) 426-8426
(Available at Radio Shack outlets)

Stress & Shrink Health Risk (IBM-compatibles)
Shareware Outlets

Stress Management 2 ($49.50)
Total Stress Management System ($89.50)
(Apple, IBM-compatibles)
Psychological Psoftware, 12486 Brickellia Street
San Diego, CA 92129, (619) 484-8877

Vision Aerobics ($129, IBM-compatibles)
Dynavision, Inc., 10 Mechanic Street, Suite C
Red Bank,. NJ 07701, (908) 219-1916

Continuum ($49.95, IBM-compatibles)
DataEast USA Inc., 1850 Orchard Street
San Jose, CA 95125, (408) 286-7074

LifeGuard ($79.95, Macintosh)
Synchronicity ($59.95, IBM-compatibles, Macintosh)
Visionary Software, P.O. Box 69191
Portland, OR 97201, (800) 877-1832, (503) 246-6200

The Emotional Spreadsheet ($149, IBM-compatibles)
Magic Partners, 1025 Noel Drive
Menlo Park, CA 94025, (415) 323-1842

Exercise Monitoring Software
Athlete's Diary ($39.95, IBM-compatibles, Macintosh)
Stevens Creek Software, 21346 Runford Drive
Cupertino, CA 95014, (408) 725-0424

Fitness Tracker ($64.95)
Lunde Engineering Inc., 5154 North 90th Street
Omaha, NE 68134, (402) 571-2070

PC Runner's Log ($29.95, IBM-compatibles)
Positive Systems, 640 E. Purdue, Suite 201
Phoenix, AZ 85020, (800) 733-1589

Running Counts ($49, IBM-compatibles)
Perry Software Inc., P.O. Box 302
Marion, IA 52302, (319) 377-7338

UltraCoach ($44.95, IBM-compatibles)
Flite Control Corp., 10740 Kenney Street, Suite 402
Santee, CA 92071, (619) 258-3905, (800) 729-1908

Graphic Coach ($24.95, IBM-compatibles)
Dunnigan Designs, 3536 Utah Street
San Diego, CA 92104, (619) 299-0752

Chapter Six
Personal Growth Software

People usually peg the computer as a tool to promote productivity, yet the home computer can help folks get more out of life in other, less tangible ways. If some of your goals include working on personal growth and inner development, you'll find your home computer a great ally.

Computers can help you get in touch with yourself by focusing your attention inward. Your computer and you have something in common: It's fascinated by you and everything about you. It never tires of hearing about your life, fantasies or goals.

Because it's so organized, it can prod you to focus on your strengths to create a winning resume—even when you're unemployed without a friend in the world.

If you get the urge to try out "silly" pursuits like handwriting analysis or astrology, your computer will never tell (or laugh at you). And you'll find that your computer will be just as discreet in matters of the heart, once it's loaded with the proper software.

Creativity is hard to pin down. But your computer's organizing skills and artificial intelligence capabilities can help make creativity more a habit than a bolt from the blue. And the many I-Ching, numerology, and even tarot software programs around can transform your computer screen into a window on the mysterious world of archetypal symbols, a source of inspiration artists and poets have drawn on since the dawn of time. Whether these programs are used for sheer laughs or in earnest depends on you, but they definitely put home computing in another dimension.

Career-Planning Software

They say that being happy in your career is the foundation to happiness in most other areas in life. *Career Design* for the IBM-compatible will help you get the best job you can. John Crystal developed the system behind *Career Design* for *What Color Is Your Parachute?*, a renowned career-development bestseller.

As you move through 60 modules, you complete exercises that stimulate you and give you personalized feedback. Learn who you are, what you want and how to get there with your computer and this package.

Resume Software

Writing a resume that's memorable without being boastful takes some doing. Computer software designed to make you reflect on your accomplishments and qualifications can make a rough job a little easier, however. Resumes that get—and hold—employers' attention demand the organization that only your home computer can provide.

A software package for the IBM-compatible family of computers combines resume creation with an entire job-search strategy.

The Resume Kit provides several on-screen templates to get you going. The forms are already organized, and you just fill them in with the particulars of your experience, education, skills and interests. Once you're familiar with it, customizing your resume is easy. Different resume styles can be selected depending on whether you're still a student, changing careers, or seeking a career in business, computer science or academia. The program automatically adjusts fonts and works with dot-matrix or laser printers.

Perhaps the strongest feature of this program is the manual, which is packed full of interview tips, job hunting strategies, and more. For example, the manual emphasizes writing a thank-you letter after an interview: a crucial piece of advice ignored all too often. (How are we employers to know if you're still interested after the interview?)

A helpful appendix containing action words will help you add pizazz to your job descriptions. Additional resources, and even a sample cover letter, are included as well. *The Resume Kit* contains other essential job hunting aids, such as a word processor for writing cover letters, equipped with a 100,000-word spell checker.

Individual's *ResumeMaker* contains a word processor as well, including an action-words glossary that really makes you shine! A target-company database ensures you'll track all the job opportunities that are right for you.

An on-screen calendar guarantees you'll keep track of appointments and follow-ups despite the frenzy and disorientation you may be experiencing. The program has a clean feel to it with endless helpful menus and dialog boxes.

The Resume Kit offers a free, four-month listing of your resume on the International Business Network on-line career advancement network. The documentation claims that IBN is used by companies to fill thousands of positions each year. Whether these claims are true or not, every little bit helps when you're advancing your career.

On the shareware front, a program called *Apply* helps keep track of applications you've sent out for jobs, contests, grants—you name it. *Apply* works as a mini-database, storing the pertinent data and merging it with text files. You can keep records of past encounters with specific institutions, and print letters, resumes and envelopes.

A Macintosh program called *Professional Resumewriter* uses templates to cut down on effort, time, and cost in resume preparation.

Strategic-Thinking Software

Once you get the job, *Mind Strategies* will send you straight to the top. This software contains all the tools you need to set goals and meet them, ensuring your success and happiness. *Mind Strategies* consists of exercises involving many leading-edge mental techniques, including subliminal messages, visualization, relaxation, goal-setting, motivational quotations, and a review of daily accomplishments.

These tools, combined with the software's ability to graphically monitor and display goals, motivates you to succeed from the start.

The Art of Negotiation for the IBM-compatible computer will teach you what they don't in business school. This software package takes advantage of the computer's ability to view a problem from many angles. If you know what you want but aren't sure how to get it, *The Art of Negotiation* may be what you need. The package comes with a book, *Fundamentals of Negotiating*, as well as a 500-page *Negotiation Manual* and a videotape by the author, who claims to be "The Father of Contemporary Negotiation."

By the way, the ability to negotiate for what you want is a skill you can carry through in many areas of life, not just on the job. Just imagine yourself impressing all and sundry with your savvy bargaining skills at the next garage sale you hit.

Love and Relationship Skill–Building Software

Compatibility Prober, for IBM-compatibles, asks you to complete a questionnaire. In turn, it assesses the compatibility of any two people, in any relationship (friends, co-workers, lovers) you choose. The program then seeks to work out a strategy to optimize the relationship.

This program's power comes from the computer's ability to store more data than the average human mind. It combines and recombines separate facts on the individuals, and reports them with more than 243,000 words of textual information at its command. Discover the diamond in the rough by letting your computer go to work on the people you know.

Lets say you've met your dream mate at last. And now you're making wedding plans. *The Wedding Planner* program can keep you sane by handling all the details (giving you more time to be the radiant couple).

The Wedding Planner tracks your budget (even your computer may have a hard time with this one!). It records gifts and guests and even prints mailing labels for all those thank-you notes. (Miss Manners says that everything should always be written by hand, in black ink. But then again, she has all the time in the world since she probably has nothing to do all day but be polite. And who's going to trust the word of someone who eats ice cream with a fork, anyway?!)

A program for Macs and IBM-compatibles called *Wedding Planner* ensures the joyous event will be a smash hit. The program contains a checklist that covers dress fitting, buying the ring, renting tuxedos and arranging for a church. Scary, huh?

If you're coming out of an unsuccessful relationship (one formed before you knew about love and relationship software), you need a good listener. After all, everyone on the job is sick of hearing about your lost love, and friends are starting to ignore your phone calls. It's time to turn to *Eliza*.

Created at MIT in 1966, *Eliza* is one of the world's celebrated artificial intelligence demonstration programs. Her fame is due to the fact that she was able to convince people that they were actually conversing with an intelligent being (unlike some of the more unconvincing people you meet at parties). This program is able to act as a non-directive psychotherapist (one who just sits across the room from you and says "Yes, go on. . . ."). As you type in a statement, the program responds with its own comments or questions, which usually are a subtle twist on what you just told it. (Ahh, shrinks!)

The program can sometimes prove helpful when you just need to get something off your chest. *Eliza* comes with the source code, so lovelorn programmers can customize *Eliza*'s responses with a minimum of fuss.

If even your computer can't help you out in the ways of love, a shareware program for the IBM-compatible family of computers might be able to at least terminate the relationship gracefully. *Divorce: Animated Strategy for Men* will educate men on rights and procedures (in California) to follow in case things just don't work out.

The humorous program presents a series of graphic screens along with text concerning the legal matters of divorce. The documentation warns that "since it was written by a man for other men, it does have a slight bias against women and marriage in general." Hmmmpf. And where's the *women's* edition?

Creativity Software

Are you tired of looking at a problem in the same old ways? Creativity-enhancing software programs might be able to help you take a step back to consider things in a different light.

MindLink is a brainstorming program that asks you to input a problem and then do some "wishing" to expand upon it. It takes you through idea generation, solution development, and solution formats modules until your brainstorm is capable of generating fertile ideas.

Another program typical of this genre is *The Idea Generator* for the IBM-compatible family of computers. This program, and others like it, enable fresh insights by making you isolate a problem and surround it with new concepts, generated by the computer's questions. *The Idea Generator* can be used in a group brainstorming session, because its report printing function helps everyone remember the meeting's objectives and outcome.

One of the best aids to imaginative thinking I've seen is a flaky-sounding shareware program called *Wisdom of the Ages*. The program asks you to go into dynamic mode. At the press of your return key, the program lists 10 or so concepts, like "failure," "travel," or "freedom," out of about a hundred. By highlighting the concept that interests you, a series of quotes comes on screen dealing with your chosen concept.

After the "essential" category of quotations (in chronological order) is taken care of, you get categories like "opposites," "flowers" (poems, songs, and the like about your concept) and several other filters through which to view the concept you've chosen.

You can choose a concept directly from a menu, instead of letting the program choose one randomly. This would be a great resource for a writer.

Thoughtline uses the structure of an outline to get you thinking.

An expensive and huge creativity-building program is *Idea Fisher*. It's huge because it contains megabytes of related words and phrases on hundreds of concepts. Select Denmark and up pops Denmark/People of Denmark, along with a choice of people, countries, cities, animals and more.

Choose animals, and up pops names of various Danish breeds. You get the picture: *Idea Fisher* paints a vivid picture of our world and takes lots of hard disk space to do so. But it may be just the spark a brilliant but burned-out copywriter needs to get creative juices flowing again.

Handwriting Analysis on Disk

Supposedly, the way you sign your name shows how you want to be seen by the world, while the way you write everything else shows the way you really are. Now you can explore the fascinating art of handwriting analysis via your versatile home computer.

A shareware program called, curiously enough, *Handwriting*

Analyst, asks you several questions about a person's signature and then produces a summary on that person based on your responses.

In the report you get information on physical and material drives, intellectual style, personality traits, social behavior, and vocational implications. You can display on screen, print, or write the report to a disk file. *Handwriting Analyst* lets you save the files for up to 20 signatures.

Some of *Handwriting Analyst*'s answers may be a little too close for comfort!

A commercial program for the Macintosh goes by the same name and offers most of the same features, as well.

Astrology Software

Astrology programs really show off the power of the computer. If you're into astrology, your computer's calculating abilities are a vast improvement over the old way of figuring various angles, houses, and planetary positions (by hand, with a huge table of charts and houses).

If astrology is less a hobby and more a source of laughs to you, astrology software can quickly print out friends' charts—complete with short character descriptions. Numerous astrology programs abound for every type of computer operating system.

Two publishers put out dozens of programs apiece for the Macintosh family of computers. Astrolabe, Inc. and Time Cycles Research should be contacted by mail for a catalog if you're at all interested in astrology. Astrolabe puts out the same titles for IBM-compatibles.

The people at Zephyr put out *Horoscopics II*, which will print charts in column form or in wheel graphics form. A shareware program called *Astrol95* lets a person's future star positions (transits) be calculated for up to one year. The charts generated by this program can be saved to disk, reviewed, deleted, sorted alphabetically, and compared with other charts.

The indefatigable folks at Lifestyle Software Group, in their never-ending quest to bring entertaining, affordable programs to the home computer, have their own astrology program: *Visions,*

The Complete Astrology System. Graphics of your planets, combined with several astrological systems (all warring, I might add), makes *Visions* worth the money. Best of all, this one comes with the charts of the rich and famous! Now you can probe the mysteries of Madonna; figure out Liz; predict Mick's future and more!

Biorhythm Programs

Are there times in the day when you're not feeling like yourself (or anyone else, for that matter)? Perhaps your body just naturally slows down at these times. That's what the study of biorhythms is all about. After input of your birthdate and personal information, computer biorhythm programs can calculate what the condition of your emotional, physical, and intellectual capacities will be.

I Ching, Numerology, and Other Software

So many fun, bizarre fortune-telling software packages exist for every possible computer operating system. *Oracle-East* is a modern implementation of the ancient Chinese way of fortune telling, based on the 4000-year-old book, *I Ching*, or Book of Changes. It's been used by introspective souls to seek their pathway since before the time of Confucius. Tossing coins or picking arrow sticks was the traditional method of obtaining a trigram, two of which form the hexagrams from which I Ching readings are taken. Nature and a dualistic philosophy prevail in the teachings of this ancient source of wisdom.

Numerology is the "science" of assigning numerical values to concepts and items like names. Computers are great with numbers, so why not let your computer calculate everything around you and determine whether you're in sync with the universe? Some people take numerology so seriously they'll change their names if they don't add up right. Some folks name their computers; now your computer can name you!

Tarot cards can be a lot of fun, and the graphics capabilities of the Macintosh family of computers is a perfect way to show off the cards' neat designs. *Tarot Pack* is a *HyperCard* stack containing the complete Tarot deck. Another program for the Macintosh, called *Gypsy*, tells your fortune in several ways—and your fee is still in your pocket when you quit the session.

Would you like to probe beyond waking consciousness, penetrate the inner meaning of your dreams? Perhaps you can, with your computer by your bedside. *The Dream Machine* is a tool for understanding and evaluating your dreams. By taking you through a series of questions, you can save your answers to disk and even come back to it another time with forgotten snippets remembered, etc. When completed, the questions are analyzed and shot to disk or to the screen. Interpretations can be printed out. The program can help you "gestalt, that is, to understand the total meaning of different objects in your dream," according to the manual. With a dream dictionary and several modules, this program offers an unusual way to pass a few hours in contemplation of the beyond.

Sources for Personal Growth Software

Career Planning Software
Career Design ($99, IBM-compatibles)
Career Design Software, P.O. Box 95624
Atlanta GA 30347, (404) 321-6100, (800) 346-8007

Resume Software
The Resume Kit ($39.95, IBM-compatibles)
Spinnaker Software Corp., One Kendall Square
Cambridge, MA 02139, (617) 494-1200, (800) 826-0706

ResumeMaker ($49.95, IBM-compatibles)
Individual Software Inc., 125 Shoreway Road, Suite 3000
San Carlos, CA 94070-2704
(800) 331-3313 (outside CA), (415) 595-8855

Apply (Disk #1005) (IBM-compatibles)
PC-SIG, 1030 East Duane Avenue, Suite D
Sunnyvale, CA 94086, (800) 245-6717 (USA), (408) 730-9291

Professional Resumewriter ($100, Macintosh)
Bootware Software Co., Inc., 28024 Dorothy Drive
Agoura Hills, CA 91301, (818) 706-3887

Strategic-Thinking Software
Mind Strategies ($129.95, IBM-compatibles)
Lightning Creative, (800) 447-0477

The Art of Negotiating ($195, IBM-compatibles)
Experience in Software, Inc., 2000 Hearst Avenue
Berkeley CA 94709, (510) 644-0694, (800) 678-7008

Love and Relationship Skill–Building Software
Compatibility Prober ($49.95, IBM-compatibles)
Neurolytic Systems, 66 Bouet Road, Suite 325
San Mateo, CA 94402, (415) 573-9001, (800) 447-0477

The Wedding Planner ($49.95, IBM-compatibles)
Ninga Software Corp., P.O. Box 215, Station "G"
Calgary, Alberta, Canada T3A 2G2, (800) 265-5555

Wedding Planner ($10, Macintosh)
Heizer Software, 1941 Oak Park Blvd., Suite 30
Pleasant Hill, CA 94523, (415) 943-7667

Eliza ($45, Apple, IBM-compatibles)
Artificial Intelligence Research Group, 921 N. La Jolla Ave.
Los Angeles, CA 90046, (213) 656-7368

Divorce (Disk #886) (IBM-compatibles)
PC-SIG, 1030 East Duane Avenue, Suite D
Sunnyvale, CA 94086, (800) 245-6717 (USA), (408) 730-9291

Creativity Software
MindLink ($299, IBM-compatibles, Macintosh)
MindLink, Inc., (800) 447-0477

Wisdom of the Ages
Shareware Distribution Channels

Idea Generator Plus ($195, IBM-compatibles)
Thoughtline ($129)
Experience in Software, 2000 Hearst Avenue
Berkeley, CA 94709, (415) 644-0694

Idea Fisher ($595)
Fisher Idea Systems, Inc., 18881 Von Karman Avenue
Irvine, CA 92715, (714) 474-8111

Handwriting Analysis on Disk
Handwriting Analyst ($6, IBM-compatibles)
PC-SIG, 1030 East Duane Avenue, Suite D
Sunnyvale, CA 94086, (800) 245-6717 (USA), (408) 730-9291

Handwriting Analyst ($69.95, Macintosh)
Wintergreen Software, 606 Webster Street
New Orleans, LA 70118, (800) 321-9479

Astrology Software

(Send for Catalog; Macintosh)
Time Cycles Research, 27 Dimmock Road
Waterford, CT 06385, (203) 444-6641

(Send for Catalog; Macintosh)
Astrolabe, Inc., P.O. Box 28, 45 S. Orleans Road
Orleans, MA 02653

Visions ($39.95, IBM-compatibles, Macintosh)
Lifestyle Software Group, (800) 289-1157

Horoscopics II ($29.95, IBM-compatibles)
Zephyr Services, 1900 Murray Avenue
Pittsburgh, PA 15217, (412) 422-6600

Astrol96 (Disk #966) (IBM-compatibles)
PC-SIG, 1030 East Duane Avenue, Suite D
Sunnyvale, CA 94086, (800) 245-6717 (USA), (408) 730-9291

Biorhythm Programs

Bio*Data ($19.95, IBM-compatibles)
Zephyr Services, 1900 Murray Avenue
Pittsburgh, PA 15217, (412) 422-6600

Biorhythm Calculator ($5, Macintosh)
Heizer Software, 1941 Oak Park Blvd., Suite 30
Pleasant Hill, CA 94523, (415) 943-7667

Biorhythm Monthly Schedule Report
Bill McGinnis Software, P.O. Box 2543
Alexandria, VA 22301 (shareware)

I Ching, Numerology, and Other Software

Oracle-East ($24.95, IBM-compatibles)
Zephyr Services, 1900 Murray Avenue
Pittsburgh, PA 15217, (412) 422-6600

Numberscope ($19.95, IBM-compatibles)
Zephyr Services, 1900 Murray Avenue
Pittsburgh, PA 15217, (412) 422-0000

Personal Numerology ($39.95, Macintosh)
Astrolabe, Inc., P.O. Box 28, 45 S. Orleans Road
Orleans, MA 02653, (508) 896-5081

Tarot Pack ($25, Macintosh)
Heizer Software, 1941 Oak Park Blvd., Suite 30
Pleasant Hill, CA 94523, (415) 943-7667

The Dream Machine ($49.50, Apple II Series, IBM-compatibles)
Psychological Psoftware Co., 12486 Brickellia
San Diego, CA 92129, (619) 484-8877
(If this type of program interests you, by all means send
away for their catalog)

Chapter Seven
The Learning Tool: Educational Software

Someone once said, "Education is what remains after people forget everything they learned in school." But education doesn't necessarily begin with that fearful first walk through the playground, nor should it end with the last dying strains of "Pomp and Circumstance."

Sure, you've been meaning to take that Chinese class after work, but the phrase "continuing education" always summons up the horrors of hunting for a parking place before night school, or trying to stoop low enough to reach the drinking fountains at adult education sites.

If you have a home computer, your worries are over. Lessons and tutorials abound, all in the convenience of your own computer room—and for a fraction of an extension course's cost. Learning is a lifelong process. With the right software, your computer can guide and inspire you in that process.

Remember, any experience can be viewed as educational under the right circumstances. Learning can take place even with "non-educational" software, like games. The most important thing is to use your imagination. View each new software package you come across as a possible learning resource. Some of the most interesting packages I've encountered defy categorization, yet are educational nonetheless.

Tasks for Educational Software

■ Learn History

■ Brush up on Domestic and International Etiquette

■ Study Foreign Cities and New Cultures

■ Learn a Foreign Language

■ Memorize the Constellations

■ Learn the Bible

■ Increase Typing Speed

■ Improve Reading, Math and Writing Skills

History Software

Whether you choose to call *Footprints in History* a game, database or educational program, this unique software package helps you learn history. It encourages family togetherness, too. When an individual or family's personal events are entered into its historical database, *Footprints in History* generates a custom time line, and places you in the wider context of world history.

Simply sit Aunt Mary down at the next family reunion, quiz her on important milestones in her life, like high school graduation, engagement to Uncle Carl, etc., and enter her data in her own VIP file on disk. Then run off an archive combining her own events with those of the world.

Imagine how thrilled she'll be to see Gandhi's 200-mile march protesting salt tax in India, March 11, 1930—right next to the entry showing the day Cousin Elmo was born! And the whole family can gather 'round the printout and play "remember when?", making Aunt Mary's time line the hit of the reunion.

Footprints in History is the perfect party or reunion ice-breaker, with the potential to spark hours of rewarding discussions and trips down memory lane for the entire family.

Time lines can be generated for a business or club as well as for individuals and families. Choose from several categories of historical events: international events, U.S. history, strange events, arts and entertainment, business, technology, and sports. Imagine generating a "Great Events in Technology" time line for a budding computer nerd, starting with his or her birthday and ending with a prize-winning science fair entry!

That Singular Day

If a time line spanning 1850 to the present is too much, *Footprints in History*'s publishers have put out a sister program,

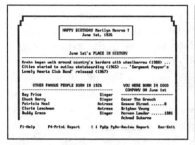 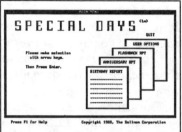

Single out that special day for a loved one.

Special Days, that can spotlight memorable days for friends or
family members. Using *Special Days* is easy. Just insert the
personal data (person's name, birthdate, anniversary date) into the
program, and seconds later a display of trivia relating to that date
appears on screen. Push a single key and an impressive printout is
generated—complete with line-borders if your printer supports
them. Kids and adults alike will marvel to find out what else was
happening the day Grandpa was born, Mom and Dad married, or
Sis won the Nobel Laureate. With a supply of parchment computer
paper, thoughtful gifts suitable for framing can be created quickly.

Footprints in History and *Special Days* engage as educational
tools because they blend personal history with "official" history—
the best way to learn.

Travel and Travel Etiquette Software

Software doesn't have to dwell in the past in order to be
educational. With specialty software like *RSVP*, you can refine
your knowledge of current mores and manners in the privacy of
your own computer room. *RSVP* asks you to navigate your way
through key social and business situations—and if you pick up the
wrong fork during your computer session, no one but your keyboard need know.

Miss Manners On-Line

RSVP lets you mind your Ps and Qs in two modes: game mode,
or straight drill and practice. If you choose game mode, you're then

asked to select a career. The first four career choices unfold in a domestic setting, while the last four let you make a fool out of yourself in countries all over the world. Depending on how you call each etiquette situation, you either rise meteorically in your chosen career or fail dismally, destined to a life of slurping soup with your dessert spoon.

The game mode offers one tiny catch: You need a good memory. From time to time an appointment book or note message flashes on screen, informing you of facts like, Mr. Smith hates cats but loves dogs. Consider yourself warned when you blow it and drag Fluffy along to that networking breakfast!

The drill mode is an effective way to hammer down the manners of a particular country before a trip—whether for business or pleasure. Selecting national situations displays a menu of 17 categories ranging from "Telephone Manners" to "Men and Women" to "Weekends Out." And for those with dinner napkin tucked firmly under chin, never fear—the "Table Manners" category is followed closely by the "More Table Manners" category.

RSVP helps you keep in mind the basic tenet of manners—consideration for others—and does so with a sense of humor. While polishing their veneers, players will learn the fascinating customs and quirks of 19 foreign nations. Now, in which country was it a must to show enjoyment of a meal by burping . . . ?

Traveling Light

Now you've got those weird customs down, thanks to *RSVP*. But if you really want to familiarize yourself with a particular country, a new breed of travel simulation software can help you learn more about that nation's art, geography, food, wine, banking, transportation, shopping, and even a bit of the language.

Ticket to Paris, and its sister programs *Ticket to London*, *Ticket to Spain*, and *Ticket to Washington, D.C.* (what language do you learn for that one?) challenge you to learn your way around and overcome various travel situations while solving a puzzle.

The *Ticket to Paris* scenario unfolds as follows: Your family has begged you to travel to Paris and track down an errant cousin who refuses to come back home. Unless you bone up on French

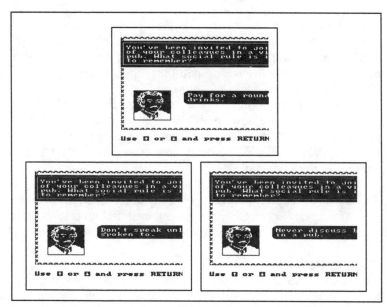

Learn how to handle yourself when drinking in Australia, with *RSVP*.

life and culture, your chances of finding the roving relative are slim. The program has you holding conversations and answering questions, using money wisely, visiting restaurants and museums, and being rewarded for your new experiences with clues. Don't forget to pay your hotel bill! (How come *my* family never sends me on such missions?)

One aspect of *Ticket to Paris* seems ridiculous. A rather moronic hunger-and-fatigue module requires you to pay attention to your physical well-being by resting enough and remembering to consume at least 24 nutritional points per day. The time clock ticks away relentlessly, and if you happen to forget to eat, you end up in the hospital.

Now, I ask you, who could forget to eat in *Paris*?

Another drawback is the constant barrage of questions greeting you at every hotel lobby or bistro. The questions are rarely in context, they're difficult, and you only get two tries. Since scoring points (and finding your cousin) depends on correctly answering the pesky woman relentlessly firing questions at you out of the blue, it would have been nice if the software program included a booklet or text file discussing question topics in the context of French history, geography, and culture.

I missed many of the more obscure questions. And having traveled to France a few times, lived there one summer, and minored in French in college, I can only imagine the frustration this game would hold for someone immersing themselves in the culture for the first time.

These are minor drawbacks in an otherwise excellent package. Those who are eagerly preparing for a trip abroad, as well as those who are eagerly staying home for some rest and relaxation, will enjoy this version of armchair (computer chair?) travel.

Conquer Jet Lag

Even with *RSVP*, it's hard to be polite when you're reeling with jet lag. When you travel, you end up turning in for the night at the most inconvenient times!

Low tech! Bring your computer power to bear on the unbearable after-effects of travel with *TimeZone: The No Jet Lag Computer System.*

The authors did plenty of research and decided that jet lag results from a combination of direction traveled, your regular sleep schedule and the number of time zones you crossed in your trip. The program takes these factors into consideration, along with current research in the effects of sunlight and diet in your destination time zone, to help you avoid jet lag at all costs.

Geography Software

Thanks to the programs just mentioned, you'll be able to get along in any foreign country (if you can find it, that is!) Most Americans are horribly deficient at geography. Europeans aren't much better. *PC-Globe* and *PC USA* to the rescue!

PC Globe is an electronic atlas that provides users with instant profiles of 190 countries and dependencies in a single, simple-to-use source. Click on a country for a detailed map, graphs and charts, facts and figures to satisfy even the most rabid geography nut. Curious about a country's flag? Click! There it is, in full color if your monitor supports it. How about the national anthem? Click, and it's sing-along time!

My co-worker, a very well-traveled man and a world-affairs newshound, keeps a copy on his Mac during sessions with his *National Geographic*. He loves the economic maps and population figures. The national anthems are true to form, proclaims another co-worker who hails from Puerto Rico. Because it's on disk, *PC Globe* can keep up with map updates more efficiently than a "hardcopy" globe or map.

What *PC Globe* does for the world, *PC USA* does for the States. For business users, the program includes detailed statistical data on major cities, average retail sales, per capita incomes and more. It allows you to pinpoint areas by area code, even zip code.

For travelers, *PC USA* offers state tourist attractions, city climate charts, and distances between cities, to mention just a few features. The publishers also make *GeoQuiz* and *GeoPuzzle USA*, kid-oriented educational programs. Traveling hats off to these fine programs that bring a world of excitement and fun to your home computer.

Once you've checked out *PC USA*, you'll hop in your car and set off—for where, and how do you get there?

Automap will set up a trip itinerary, detailed road maps, sites to visit along the way, for any route in the continental United States. There are maps of 359,220 freeways in there: Load it on the laptop and let's get going!

Ah, I almost forgot. These aren't the freewheelin' days of old Route 66. There's gridlock in them thar hills, but never fear: *Automap* knows the trouble spots between any two major destinations, and can advise alternate routes. Whew! The wind in our hair, the open road before us once again, thanks to *Automap*.

Foreign Language Programs

Loaded with the right foreign language software, your computer will compare only to your seventh-grade Spanish teacher in its steadfast determination to drill a new language into your brain.

If you haven't yet studied a foreign language, computer software can be a firm, yet patient, teacher. And if you just need a little practice for that upcoming trip, dozens of language programs can show you how to ask where the bathroom is with finesse.

Hola, Bonjour, Guden Tag

Combining the best features of databases and word processors, a good language program can conjugate any verb, give noun forms and genders, give tips on style and usage, and even search and replace from English into the acquired language.

One set of programs, MicroTac's *Language Assistant* software, even offers an accent-entry feature, where you just hit a hot-key combination (Control-'), the letter you want accented, and the accent mark. Voilà, a freshly accented character pops up right in the middle of your word processor document.

These programs have grown immensely in sophistication and features: Now you can even type a letter in English and a *Micro-Tac* program will attempt a translation! Great software from a winning team. Most language programs come with complete verb conjugations. Having every verb tense, form, and person available at the touch of a key is something I would have killed for in college. (Then again, a computer would have been handy in college, too.) The Macintosh desk accessory *Le conjugueur*'s sole purpose in life is to supply the correct conjugation of all the French verbs.

Designed for those who use French often in their work or study, this program is a must.

The MicroTac *Language Assistant* programs mentioned above supply a complete explanation of each verb tense's use, at the touch of a function key. Now you can finally discover the purpose of those 50 Spanish subjunctive tenses.

Bilingual dictionaries are almost always included in full-featured language programs. By typing either the English or target-language word in the *Language Assistant* programs, the translation pops up on the screen.

Synonyms are no problem. For the English word "slip," for example, you get the foreign translation for the woman's under-garment and the verb "to slip." The memory-resident mode lets you hit the <Enter> key from within your word processor and the translation sticks itself right into your document.

On the public domain front, *Language Teacher* is a series of menu-driven language tutorial programs designed to be run on IBM-compatibles. Each program in the series contains hundreds of word combinations and verb conjugation forms.

The program lets you select language-to-English or English-to-language combinations, multiple-choice answers, and retesting when you miss an answer. You can print a multiple-choice test, and run a full quiz diagnostic routine with line printer output. Of particular interest to non-English-speaking students is the option to select the direction of the combinations.

All word, phrase, and verb conjugation selections are randomly generated by the program, so the user is unable to predict the next selection. The program package is not designed to teach conversational language or pronunciation; rather, it provides practice drills in order to increase your working vocabulary and to enhance your use of the conjugation forms.

I tried out the "Spanish I" module, and although the vocabulary words were easy, I found myself trying to race the time clock—and enjoying every minute. Good practice, especially for the program's price: free.

Where Were You on the Night of the . . .

Another foreign language program that makes learning fun is *Whodunit* for the Mac. You can solve a mystery in either French, German, or Spanish, by choosing the right answers when the program asks you questions. (Don't worry; the butler did it.)

Astronomy Software

Foreign language software can help you travel the world, but wouldn't it be nice to be able to travel to other worlds? You can, merely by loading an astronomy software package into your home computer. Think of how prepared you'll be when Earth is overtaken by extraterrestrials.

Orbits: Voyage Through the Solar System lets you zoom around the graphically precise, full-color solar system, and get a meteor-eye view of the universe. This interactive space simulator and space atlas, by the makers of *Automap* and *Bodyworks*, has got to be seen. Great animations and color graphics really take advantage of that color monitor you've been meaning to pick up.

With *Orbits*, you can run simulations of the planet's motions, watch eclipses, the nuclear processes of the Sun, tides, the Moon's orbit, or even simulate the birth and death of the Sun. Neat, huh? This one's a must on any educational software shelf.

Most astronomy programs are based on celestial databases. Generally, you can focus in on various galactic phenomena, or check out the sky for any given date. One astronomy program, *Voyager* for the Macintosh, really shines.

At the heart of the *Voyager* astronomy program is its 14,000-object database, including 9,100 stars, 3,000 deep-space objects (galaxies, etc.), 88 constellation outlines, the planets in our solar system, and more. Not only can you view the night sky from anywhere on earth (specifying either one of 135 earthly cities, or any longitude and latitude) but also from any planet. You can even get really weird and view the sky from deep space. The sky can be viewed as a star chart and a celestial sphere, as well.

You get to select your point of view from time, as well as from space. *Voyager* can display the heavens on any date from 1000 B.C. to A.D. 4000. If any planet, star, or nebula sparks further interest, you can click on it and up pops a data box. The box tells you more about its name, Yale number, type, distance, magnitude, location coordinates—everything you ever wanted to know about that celestial object but were afraid to ask.

Software publisher Zephyr Services offers a whole range of astronomy programs. Space allows mention of only a few; if you're a dedicated astronomer, you should write away for its catalog.

Astrofinder offers skyviews for your date, time, and location, and lets you filter out lesser star magnitudes to make the display easier to see. With a deep-sky object file, you can add and delete comets, planets and other space objects. Zephyr's *Suntracker* calculates astronomical conditions for any solar eclipse and displays a map with areas of visibility. The program computes and provides eclipse elements, accurate to 12 miles on the Earth's surface. The program lets you input your own elements to achieve greater accuracy, as well.

Moontracker does the same thing, but for lunar eclipses. *Cometwatch* teaches all about comets, how and when to observe them, and even how to photograph them. *Astrocalc* features all the basic astronomical data for any date and location.

Have you ever gone out to the desert, looked up at the night sky, and wished you knew the names of all those stars? Zephyr's *Astrostell* teaches the various constellations, their lore, and the stars that comprise them. You can see the more common star formations, have the program pick constellations at random and quiz you for their names, or select among the 88 specific constellations listed. The program also offers hints on how to get started stargazing, and teaches the history of constellation discovery as well as the history of star mapping.

Bible Software

Gazing at the heavens through your computer screen may inspire you to *ponder* the heavens through your computer screen. What better means to finding out the meaning of it all than loading your computer with Bible software? Even if your beliefs lie outside the Judeo/Christian tradition, the Bible is a valuable source of wisdom, inspiration, and just plain good reading.

What's the advantage to having the Bible on your computer? Bible software typically offers the entire Bible in the form of a database, making it easy to search for a particular word or combination of words. You can also search for specific sections or verses. Listings of all that word's or phrase's appearances come up instantaneously. This makes it easy to trace an idea or theme throughout the Bible.

The Bible program *WORDsearch*, for the MS-DOS family, is especially helpful for people who may use a computer as a tool, but not as a hobby in itself. The on-screen help menus and manual are written in a non-threatening, step-by-step style. The program is capable of searching the entire Bible for a word in two seconds. Another plus is the note feature, where you can record your thoughts and studies, combine them with other notes and verses, and print them out—a real benefit to clergy or others who work regularly with the Bible.

A Macintosh program called *MacBible* takes advantage of the Mac's superior graphics capabilities by offering Bible graphics, maps, and charts, as well as a 25-disk volume of the King James Bible with chapter and verse search.

It's easy to bone up on Bible facts and figures with a shareware program for the IBM PC-compatible family called *Bible Quiz Plus*. The program is billed as a religious trivia game with three different levels of play. One to six seekers can play. Questions can be answered in multiple choice, fill-in-the-blank, or answer-only mode. The questions are from the Books of Psalms and Proverbs, and are printable. A user option lets you create your own questions. *Bible Quiz Plus* is fun to play and is a great educational tool for children and adults alike.

Another Bible program, *Scripture Bits* for the Macintosh family of computers, lets you generate a verse for every day in the year. A Topics feature lets you search for specific subjects from "Acceptance" to "Youth," arranged alphabetically. A Quotations section holds pearls of wisdom taken from the book of Acts to Zephaniah, and a Religious Charts section holds Old and New Testament chronology charts. The program is available in either English or Spanish as well. Buy the Spanish version and learn two things at once: wisdom from the Bible and a foreign language.

Those who find themselves writing often about the Bible may find the Macintosh software program *Bible Spelling Dictionary* handy. This program features a 20,000-word religious dictionary that contains all of the unique words, names, places, abbreviations and topics of the Old and New Testaments, including the obsolete spellings in the King James version of the Bible. Customizing the dictionary is easy to do in case a new archeological find in the Holy Land is uncovered by bomb blasts.

Typing Tutors

Just about every computer-adept person I've met is able to type extremely rapidly. I'm not sure which came first, the fast typing ability or the computer ability, but this can't be mere coincidence.

So, learn to type even faster and start down the road to Computer Guru-dom today.

With one of the many good typing tutor software packages out there, your computer can assess your skill level, drill you on problem areas, and even let you customize your own lessons, in the case of *Mavis Beacon Teaches Typing!*, for IBM-compatible computers.

The true advantage of computer typing tutors is their ability to automatically adjust to a user's abilities. Compare this with the old method of taking the page out of the typewriter, then circling all the mistakes you made, charting all the letters mistyped, and then turning to each of the drills focusing on those letters.

Most typing programs feature some sort of metronome or clock ticking in order to give you a sense of rhythm while pounding away on the keyboard. It's easy to disable this feature if it drives you nuts. You can also turn off and on the "guide hands" option in many programs. *Mavis Beacon* lets you save your setup preferences for the next time you use the program.

Positive feedback is important in a learning situation, and most programs display a graph or chart of your progress. *Mavis Beacon* lets you print out a report card, too. (But you don't get a chocolate coin when you do extra well, as in Madame Rigsby's sophomore French class.)

Mavis Beacon Teaches Typing! is *almost* "the finest typing program in the world," as its box proclaims. Alas, the program is copy-protected, and demands that you insert the "key" disk on and off throughout your session with the program. What a hassle.

The ability to print results gives you a personal record of the speed/accuracy goals you set. You can monitor whether or not you're actually making progress. *Typing Tutor IV* for the Macintosh has you complete a goals questionnaire that asks you about your current level of experience and desired typing speed.

On the shareware front, the *Touchtype* disk from PC-SIG (#320) for IBM-compatibles is a complete program that ranges from beginning to advanced skill levels. With CGA-quality graphics and configurable features, this program has almost as much going for it as commercial IBM-compatible programs—at a fraction of the cost.

Readin', Writin', 'rithmetic

Computers are ideal for learning esoteric stuff like international etiquette or Cantonese Chinese. But once in a while it's good to brush up on the basics, and reading, writing, and arithmetic software is the place to start. Several programs exist in each of these categories for every operating system imaginable.

College Entrance Exam Preparation Programs

Using your home computer during the course of your college career is smart. But you can start taking advantage of the computer's educational capabilities long before you're accepted to a college or university. Scholastic Aptitude Test (SAT) preparation programs exist for every type of computer operating system. The programs, all similar to each other, contain tests for each of the SAT's sections: Verbal, Math, and Logic.

The Perfect Score: Computer Preparation for the SAT for the Macintosh comes with a bonus program: a college-selection database called *The Perfect College.*

Barron's, the publishers of the familiar softcover college prep workbooks, offers an IBM-compatible preparation program with modules that analyze the student's answers and pinpoint weaknesses and strengths. *Barron's Computer Study Program for the SAT* offers tests in two modes: Testing Mode, which simulates real test conditions, and Learning Mode. Learning Mode gives you *two* chances to answer those typical SAT questions, like: If five people each wore yellow overalls except Mary, and the two named Fred lost red galoshes last Thursday, but the bus only stops at Fourth and Main at 2 p.m. every other Tuesday, what day will Easter fall on this year?

Speed-Reading Programs

Whether you're trying to get into the college of your choice, or just trying to read all the trade journals and other materials that pile up at work every week, speed reading is a great skill to acquire. The computer is ideally suited to reading instruction because words can flash across an otherwise blank screen and successfully hold your attention like no book can.

Flashread, a speed-reading program for the IBM and compatible family of computers, forces the eye to focus on three words at a time. Since the eye can transmit information to the brain only when it isn't moving, reading one word at a time results in jumpy eye movements that slow the flow of information to the brain. Practice with *Flashread* can increase peripheral vision, allowing you to read larger word groupings.

After a diagnostic test to determine your reading index number, the program enters the "linear reading" mode, where groups of three words flash across the screen at your optimum reading speed level. Your eyes are forced to fixate on the groups of words—and you begin to automatically read at your most efficient rate. When you're reading effortlessly and most efficiently, *Flashread* calls this the fusion level.

Once you hit fusion level, the linear reading mode subtly speeds up. I wanted to slow it down a tad by hitting the space bar (which you can do any time during practice), but after deciding against changing my reading index number, I re-entered practice mode again to find it had slowed by itself. Good. I was getting dizzy.

A program for the Macintosh offers eye exercises designed to strengthen muscles as well as improve movement rates. *Speed Reader II* contains six muscle-building activities.

Reading and Reasoning

Queue publishes the *Lessons in Reading* and *Reasoning I–IV* series for all the computer families. These programs teach you how to spot fallacies in what you read. You can become a more critical reader (and thinker).

Build Writing Skills

Computers may make writing easier, but what if you could use your computer to make your writing better? Many style and grammar checking programs exist. The better ones offer tips to improve your choice of words and sentence length.

Readability for IBM-compatible computers is one of the best writing aids around. Save an example of your writing as a text file, and bring it into *Readability*. Choose one of nine categories of writing you think it fits. Categories range from "Children's books" to "Magazine feature articles" to "Bureaucratic gobbledygook." You can see at a glance how your writing measures up in any of 16 diagrams. Suggestions to increase your writing's readability follow. The hardcover manual is extensive and well-researched.

Math Programs

As with so many types of educational software, math programs number in the thousands. One of the most versatile shareware programs for IBM-compatible computers is *Math Pak II*, which can bring you up to speed in everything from very basic arithmetic to calculus, trigonometry, and geometry.

Plusses and Minuses

As far as the foreign language programs go, one of the *Language Assistant* series' drawbacks is that the screen colors are not configurable. Because of incompatibility with my word processor's screen (*WordPerfect*), I had to suffer through orange text on a red background while in the memory-resident mode. Not very easy to see. The stand-alone display looked just fine.

Also, don't rely on the *Language Assistant* series' "Replace Word for Word" feature for anything other than the most basic guidelines to foreign word order, grammar, and vocabulary. Although the manual does warn that you're to use "your skills and the Assistant to refine the document" afterwards—don't bother unless that foreign language is really Greek to you. This feature was made for that panic-ridden cram night when a 10-page translation is due and you haven't cracked a book all semester. Only a desperate person would consider using it. It's *that* rough.

In matters celestial, *Astrostell* will happily list all the constellations you can see at any one time, date, and locale, but after displaying your first choice, it bounces back into the main menu and you have to start all over again by entering—you guessed it—date, time and locale. You should be able to preview, and print out if you wish, all the constellations visible that night. One way to get around this is to print the screen which lists the visible star formations for that date, and then go to the main constellation menu and select the various constellations by number.

Body Language

We've toured the world, America first; explored other cultures and languages; and rocketed to the stars. But what about that inner sanctum, our own bodies? *Bodyworks: An Adventure in Anatomy* lets you in on the ultimate educational adventure as you probe and view the entire human body in living color.

You zoom in and out of specific areas, and animations along the way graphically explain how the heart pumps blood and other functions. Observe the eye, study the brain, or take a broader view of the skeletal, muscular, nervous, reproductive or other systems. This program looks great with a VGA monitor, by the way. Extremely well done programming and graphics ensure you, and the whole family, a ready reference for years to come.

Sources for Educational Software

History Software
Footprints in History
($39.95)
Special Days
($39.95, IBM-compatibles)
The Salinon Corporation, P.O. Box 31047
Dallas, TX 75231, (800) 722-0054, (214) 692-9091

Travel and Travel Etiquette Software
RSVP Ticket to . . . series
($39.95, Apple II series, Commodore 64/128,
IBM-compatibles, Macintosh)
Blue Lion Software, 90 Sherman Street
Cambridge, MA 02140, (617) 876-2500, (800) 333-0199

TimeZone
($199, fits on average laptop; IBM-compatibles)
Management Consulting International Co.
Alan V. Cameron, Ph.D., 25 Beechwood Avenue
Irvine, CA 92714, (714) 552-4660

Geography Software
PC Globe ($69.95)
PC USA ($69.95, IBM-compatibles)
MacGlobe ($79.95, Macintosh)
GeoQuiz ($49.95)
GeoPuzzle USA ($39.95, Apple II and IBM)
PC Globe, Inc., 4700 South McClintock
Tempe AZ 85282, (800) 336-6314, (602) 730-9000

Automap ($99.95, IBM-compatibles)
Automap Inc., 9831 S. 51st Street, Bldg. C-113
Phoenix, AZ 85044, (602) 893-2400

Foreign Language Software
The Language Assistant Series ($79.95/each, IBM-compatibles)
Spanish, French, German, Italian
MicroTac Software, 4655 Cass Street, Suite 304
San Diego, CA 92109, (619) 272-5700

Le conjuguer ($49.95, Macintosh)
Les editions Ad Lib, Inc., 220 Grande Allee est, Suite 960
Quebec, Canada G1R 2J1, (418) 529-9676, (800) 463-2686

Language Teacher (free, IBM-compatibles)
Spanish, French, German, Italian
Micro Tutor Products, 103 Baughmans Lane, Suite 303
Frederick, MD 21701

Whodunit
($49.95, Macintosh, 512K and up; $49.95, IBM-compatibles)
Gessler Publishing Co., 55 W. 13th Street
New York, NY 10011, (212) 627-0099

Astronomy Programs
Orbits: Voyage Through the Solar System
($59.95, IBM-compatibles)
Software Marketing Corp., 9831 South 51st Street, Bldg. C-113
Phoenix, AZ 85044, (602) 893-2400

Voyager ($124.50, Amiga, Macintosh)
Carina Software, 830 Williams Street
San Leandro, CA 94577, (510) 352-7332

AstroFinder
($49.95, IBM-compatibles)
Suntracker
($29.95, IBM-compatibles, Apple II family, Commodore 64/128)
Astrocalc

($29.95, IBM-compatibles, Apple II family, Commodore 64/128)
Moontracker
($29.95, IBM-compatibles, Apple II family, Commodore 64/128)
Astrostell
($29.95, IBM-compatibles, Apple II family)
Cometwatch
($29.95, IBM-compatibles, Apple II family, Commodore 64/128)
Zephyr Services, 1900 Murray Avenue
Pittsburgh, PA 15217, (412) 422-6600, (800) 533-6666

Bible Software

WORDsearch ($9, IBM-compatibles; hard disk required)
WORDworks Software Architects, 5014 Lakeview Drive
Austin, TX 78732, (512) 266-9898, (800) 888-9898

MacBible ($129), *MacBible Concordance* ($75)
(Macintosh; hard disk required)
Encycloware, 712 Washington Street
Ayden, NC 28513

MacConcord I ($16.95)
MacGospel ($12.95)
MacScripture ($49.95)
Scripture Bits ($12.95)
Medina Spelling Dictionary ($16.95)
(Macintosh; hard disk required)
Medina Software, Inc., 2008 Las Palmas Circle
Orlando, FL 32822, (407) 260-1676

Typing Tutors

Mavis Beacon Teaches Typing ($49.95, IBM-compatibles)
The Software Toolworks, One Toolworks Plaza
13557 Ventura Blvd., Sherman Oaks, CA 91423, (415) 883-3000

Typing Tutor IV ($39.95, Macintosh)
Simon & Schuster Software, 1 Gulf + Western Plaza, 14th Floor
New York, NY 10023, (213) 373-8882, (800) 624-0023

PC-Fastype (Disk #320) (IBM-compatibles)
PC-SIG, 1030 East Duane Avenue, Suite D
Sunnyvale, CA 94086, (800) 245-6717 (USA), (408) 730-9291

College Entrance Exam Preparation Software

The Perfect Score: Computer Preparation for the SAT
($79.95, Macintosh)
Mindscape, Inc., 3444 Dundee Road
Northbrook, IL 60062, (800) 221-9884

SAT Score Improvement System ($99.95, Macintosh)
Spinnaker Software Corp., 1 Kendall Square
Cambridge, MA 02139, (617) 494-1222

Barron's Computer Study Program for the SAT ($49.95)
Barron's Computer Study Program for the ACT ($79.95)
(IBM-compatibles)
Barron Educational Series, 250 Wireless Blvd.
Hauggauge, NY 11788, (516) 434-3311

Reading, Writing, and Arithmetic Programs
Flashread ($49.95, IBM-compatibles)
PVA Systems, 7777 Fay Avenue, Suite K
La Jolla, CA 92037, (619) 456-0707

Speed Reader II ($69.95, Macintosh)
Davidson & Associates, Inc., 3135 Kashiwa Street
Torrance, CA 90505, (213) 534-4070, (800) 556-6141

Lessons in Reading and Reasoning I–IV
($149.95/each, Apple, IBM, Macintosh)
Queue, 562 Boston Avenue
Bridgeport, CA 06610-1705, (203) 335-0908

Readability ($25)
Corporate Voice ($295, IBM-compatibles)
Scandinavian PC Systems, Inc., 51 Monroe Street, Suite 707A
Rockville, MA 20850, (301) 294-7450

Math Pak III (Disk #394) (IBM-compatibles)
PC-SIG, 1030 East Duane Avenue, Suite D
Sunnyvale, CA 94086
(800) 222-2996 (CA), (800) 245-6717 (USA), (408) 730-9291

Bodyworks ($59.95, IBM-compatibles)
Software Marketing Corp., 9831 South 51st Street, Bldg. C-113
Phoenix, AZ 85044, (602) 893-2400

Chapter Eight

The Computer at Large: Telecommunications

While a modem is the least computer-like thing you can buy for your computer, modems and computers still have a few things in common. Modems, like computers, quickly perform routine or repetitive tasks. For example, modems can redial phone numbers in a flash. And modems are able to record keystrokes and play them back later, just like computer programs with macro capabilities. But buying a modem and going on-line lets you meet and communicate with people—something most computer applications don't offer at all.

Once you've equipped your computer with a modem and some communications software, your computer can call local and national BBSs, or Bulletin Board Systems. Hobbyists just like you and me have set up computers in their own homes and equipped them with modems and bulletin board software so that other people with modems can call and leave messages (just like a "real" bulletin board), play games, discuss issues, download software—the possibilities are endless. Zillions of bulletin board systems are waiting for you to call. Each has its distinct personality and population. Once you find some bulletin board systems you like, you'll see the camaraderie and entertainment a modem can bring to your life. (The free software alone is worth the price of a modem.)

Having a modem and some communications software for your computer can enhance your computer hobby in more ways than just meeting people over the phone lines. With a subscription to a commercial on-line service (kind of like a big, national BBS where you're billed for the time you spend on-line), you can shop, book airline tickets, advance your career, manage your money, play games, and more. In fact, no matter where your interests lie, a modem can make you wonder how you ever got along without one.

Do you long to play a good game of chess, but hate the trek over to your chess buddy's house across town? A modem and special modem gaming software for your computer lets you checkmate your opponent without seeing the sore loser's wrath in person. If chess or checkers aren't gory enough for you, many best-selling commercial computer games have begun offering the ability to play on-line (as long as your opponent also has a copy of the game software, along with a modem).

If you've always wanted to work at home, a modem and some remote access computer software can make this dream come true. These "remote control" packages give you the ability to control, monitor, and test software running on a PC somewhere else. You can transfer all your work files to your home computer from the comfort of home, and the donuts and coffee are handier.

We've all heard the computer experts predicting the day of the "paperless" office. But you'd probably like to see the day of the paperless home. This fantasy can be one step closer to reality with software that enables electronic banking. Imagine never having to write a paper check again—never mind messing with stamps, licking envelopes, and trying to find those freebie return address labels that charities are always sending you.

Tasks for Modems & Telecommunications Software

- Call Bulletin Board Systems
- Join Commercial On-Line Services
- Play Games by Modem
- Remote Computing, or Work From Home
- Bank From Home

Calling Bulletin Board Systems

There is a BBS (Bulletin Board System, or "board") for every personality and interest imaginable. A quick glance at any local computer magazine's BBS list reveals boards devoted to every type of computer hardware configuration, as well as to such diversities as finance, surfing, and even genealogy.

Meeting people "on-line" who think the way you do and are willing to communicate is often described as a sort of "high." But before you sit down and program every Bulletin Board System you see into your communication program's dialing directory, you should look for a program that can help you save money and time.

Many local BBSs carry Telephone Prefix Checker utility programs that tell which prefixes are long distance or toll calls. You won't find these programs listed in the back of this chapter, because they are written by telecommunication enthusiasts with a specific city's telephone prefixes in mind.

The best place to find handy programs like these is on a BBS —since people who run BBSs naturally have an interest in tele-communications programs of all kinds. You can quickly download (get the BBS computer to send it to your computer) these programs because they're small.

Prefix checker utility programs ask for your home phone's prefix (or the phone from which you're modeming) and the prefix of the BBS you want to call. The checker instantly tells you where the bulletin board system is located and whether or not calling it will cost you anything. Even if you've lived in your city all your life, a program like this comes in handy for pinpointing unfamiliar prefixes. Most of these programs are quick and colorful. Best of all, you don't have to sit there with the White Pages in your lap, checking each number against the prefix chart.

These prefix checkers work at any stage in the calling process. Whether you're wondering whether to call a BBS, or you find yourself in the middle of one and decide that downloading that 320K graphics demo just isn't worth it (especially if you find out the BBS is in the outer reaches of your county), the prefix checker pops right up.

Once you find a BBS that isn't a toll call and call it up, you'll probably be asked to think of a password for future log-ons. Rather than jotting your secret password on the nearest scrap of paper—or worse, *not* jotting it down at all—use your computer's filing skills to keep track of things.

Note: Use a different password for each system you log onto. If a BBS's user list is broken into by malicious pranksters, you could experience great chaos and confusion, not only there but on every system you call.

Most BBSs have some telecommunications utilities that print a form to help you remember what you did during a call to a BBS. Many of these have blanks where you can fill in the date and time you last called a BBS, the names of people with whom you exchanged messages, what you downloaded and uploaded, and password and user I.D. records—all jotted down in one place.

Some BBSs are distinctive. You can tell right away what kind of people inhabit the board and if you feel comfortable there.

Other BBSs are harder to figure: Either there isn't much happening, or you haven't put enough time into finding out. The same holds true for users too, and that's why the sysop of a BBS will often ask a new user to write an on-line letter telling a little about himself or herself before he or she can obtain an "account" there.

What you do or don't reveal in the letter will sometimes motivate the sysop to give you a higher or lower level of access on the BBS. Generally, the higher your access, the more time you can spend on-line. With higher access you'll be participating in more discussion areas and file directories and better games. It's best to be yourself in the letter. Don't be afraid to go into some detail about your life, interests, and goals. After all, it's the neighborly thing to do, and remember, you're there to meet people.

Nobody likes a slug, and sysops are no exception. That's why your access level increases with the number of discussions in which you participate. The number of shareware programs you upload also counts big with sysops. A bulletin board's vitality is quickly drained when everybody who logs on just reads personal messages, downloads a couple of games, and logs off.

Once you find a system that appeals to you, try to participate fully in the main board and the various discussion forums (sometimes known as "conferences" or "sub-boards"). Upload articles you think others would enjoy reading. If you make your presence known, you just might be stimulated, challenged, or enlightened.

But you have to put energy into on-line communications to get anything back.

Due to the monstrous proportions media-hype has given the on-line phenomenon, it's hard to remember that most of those bizarre BBS names on that list represent a variety of groups of people striving for communication. So have fun! The decisions about what modem or communications software to buy are just the beginning of the choices you'll make in the on-line world.

Commercial On-Line Services

Commercial on-line services seem to sprout as fast as BBSs. And, as with BBSs, there are many flavors of commercial on-line services from which to choose. Most of them offer similar services, however, like on-line shopping, travel reservations, news, weather, sports, discussion areas, software downloading, and games.

Although this book is not intended to recommend one service over another, since they change so rapidly, I'd still like to express my gratitude for Prodigy Services. My time on Prodigy has been enjoyable, educational, touching—as well as invaluable as an aid in compiling this book (to see what types of home software people were *really* using). If you've never tried it out, you might send off for a starter kit and fire 'er up.

Throughout the other chapters in this edition, you'll find bulletin boards and commercial services mentioned as great sources for information or software in certain areas of interest. Take the plunge and buy a modem. I can't tell you how much you'll get out of it.

Socializing On-Line Is Fun

You can increase your social circle rapidly when you join a commercial on-line service. They all offer on-line communications centers, with fast, inexpensive means of communicating with business associates, friends old and new, and family. You can send letters, documents, or your latest recipe through whatever electronic messaging system the commercial on-line service happens to use. Some of the commercial on-line services offer electronic CB simulators.

This feature can be an expensive waste of time or a novel experience, depending on how you look at it.

Money Matters

Banking and brokerage services, annual reports of major corporations, business news, stock market quotes, and forums on everything from personal finance to investing in baseball cards are offered by most of the commercial on-line services. Some of the services actually let you buy, sell, and trade in the stock market 24 hours a day.

You can learn to handle money more wisely. There are services that let you calculate interest payments and mortgage schedules, balance your checkbook, and figure your net worth.

Improve Your Chances

With the help of a commercial on-line service you can access any sort of industry-related information. This can be a big asset in furthering your career. Forums are available for lawyers, entrepreneurs, journalists—you name it. Resumes and job opportunities are often listed in special areas. Now you can let the experts give you career tips and advice.

The vast array of databases offered by most commercial on-line services lets you quickly add current information to reports, proposals, and even term papers. The news features offered by the commercial on-line services guarantee that your data will never be stale or erroneous.

Educational Resources

Many of the commercial on-line services offer on-line editions of encyclopedias and other reference materials. Rather than getting stuck with a soon-to-be-outmoded set of encyclopedias, access current information on-line. The many reference areas and databases offered by these services are essential educational tools. You can pick up information in the various discussion areas, too.

Computer-related discussion areas are almost as numerous as types of computers. You can learn as much or as little about your particular setup as you want. Industry experts can be accessed through electronic messaging capabilities. In fact, most of the commercial on-line services offer forums hosted by the big software publishers, so you can complain right on-line about that obscure software manual. Computer publications like *Dr. Dobb's Journal* and *Computer Language* can be found on some of the bigger commercial on-line services, like CompuServe.

News, Weather, and Sports

Many of the commercial on-line services subscribe to the Associated Press News and Sports wires, as well as various weather services and business news services. Or, there are smaller, more specialized commercial on-line services devoted only to weather, news, or sports.

Fun and Games

The larger commercial on-line services offer news, reviews, and up-to-date dirt on the doings of the rich and famous. Some of the services even offer daily soap opera summaries.

If gaming is what you're after, you can play arcade space-war, word and trivia, or fantasy-adventure games. One drawback is that you're getting charged for every minute you spend on-line.

Discussion areas of the larger on-line services offer news of comic books, electronics, music, sci-fi, and other entertainment doings. Hobby forums are fun to explore as well. Joining a commercial on-line service can ensure hours of entertainment.

Health and Nutrition

The more general commercial on-line services offer health-oriented databases. Since experts belong to the discussion forums, you can obtain up-to-date guidance on diet, first aid, preventive medicine, and more. Some of the commercial on-line services even offer support groups centering around such areas as substance abuse and living with cancer.

Many discussion forums offered by the larger commercial on-line services focus on gourmet cooking and good restaurants.

Shop, But Not 'Til You Drop

Shopping in a giant electronic mall can be yours, 24 hours a day, with a membership in one of the larger commercial on-line services. Many well-known retailers and manufacturers have set up shop on the commercial on-line services. Some of the services offer discount shopping as well. Now you too can have the UPS guy blazing a trail to your door.

If travel is in your future, you can shop airfares, hotels, and tours with the travel features offered by the larger commercial on-line services. Once you find a fare or hotel rate that suits your budget, you can access air schedules and make reservations. Tickets can be picked up at your local travel agent or received by mail.

Before an overseas journey, you can check with CompuServe's Department of State's Travel Advisory Service for information about international currencies, vaccination and visa requirements, as well as customs regulations.

How Much Does It Cost?

Specific costs for each commercial on-line service change too rapidly to mention here. The on-line services have similar pricing structures, however. You pay an initial membership fee ranging from $25 to $50 for the more general services. You're then billed for any time you spend on-line, roughly $6 to $15 an hour. Some of the services charge a small monthly fee after the first three months of membership. Any travel arrangements you make are billed to your credit card, as well.

Each on-line service is listed in the back of this chapter. They all have toll-free numbers, and they'll be happy to answer questions about current fees and services.

Telecommunications Software

Once you've bought a modem, you'll need telecommunications software. Most of the software programs have similar features. Describing the many individual communications software packages available for each operating system would be redundant. Instead, here's a list of features you should look for in a communications package.

Make sure your communications package is easily configurable to your particular modem speed (the speed at which the computer you want to call is running) and other variables you may want to alter from time to time. Rigid software is the last thing you need. You'll want the software to provide a dialing directory, too, where you can add all the numbers you call and get your computer to automatically dial and redial the numbers at the touch of a key.

A good communications program will offer a wide range of protocols for uploading and downloading files. Protocols are the actual file-transfer programs that ensure your data is being transmitted in the most optimal method possible. *QModem SST* for the IBM-compatible family of computers is superior in this area because it lets you add new, or "external," protocols as soon as they're developed. Since telecommunications programs and utilities are constantly being improved upon, being able to add new protocols is the best way to stay current. While on the subject of uploading and downloading files, make sure the process is easily accessible. Some programs let you upload or download in batches, allowing for the transfer of several files at one time.

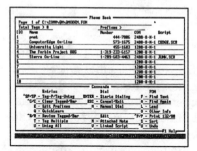

Typical of a dialing directory, *QModem*'s phone book lists BBSs you call frequently.

You'll want to automate more than just the actual dialing and redialing process. Find a communications program that has a Quick Learn feature, so all your keystrokes on a particular BBS are memorized and a script, or

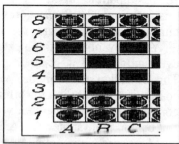

Play chess with a remote opponent with telegaming software.

giant macro, can be automatically generated. That way, next time you call, the script goes into effect automatically and you just kick back while your computer does all the work of logging in and joining conferences.

You can take the automation process to the extreme by having the computer actually call the BBS by itself, log on, download all

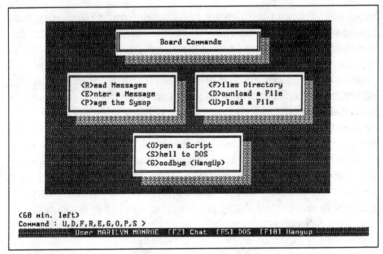

QModem's host mode displays a menu to folks calling your computer.

the mail waiting for you, upload any mail you want to send, and log off. This is great for calling BBSs in other cities when phone rates are cheapest. Top-notch programs have timer capabilities that make this feature easy. Other programs, such as the shareware IBM-compatible program called *The Brain*, are devoted only to this function. *The Brain* works by building a command file containing special commands the program enacts in your absence.

You may not use this next feature much as a beginner, but eventually you'll want other computers to be able to call yours. This is called "host mode," and most of the good shareware communications programs offer it. This lets you access your own computer from anywhere, or your friends can call your computer and upload that rad new VGA demo they've been raving about.

Make sure your communications program has a capture buffer, so you can save important messages or other information. Also, being able to access your disk operating system while in the communications software is important.

Finally, try to find a communications program with a good on-line help screen. Good shareware programs should come with a manual you can print out (be wary, though, the *QModem* manual has hundreds of pages and takes forever to print, and if you register the program and send a little extra, they'll mail you a really nice, typeset manual).

Gaming With Your Modem

It's 2025, violence has been outlawed, and the Sport of WAR, played by robots and based on the 20th Century game of football, is the most popular game in town. A modem version of the game has been developed for those with "a little concentration, a little dedication, and a lot of desire to pound your opponent into cube steak." So opens the futuristic manual to *Modem Wars*, a computer game with a twist.

Unlike most computer games, played in the solitude of your computer room, *Modem Wars* is played by two people. You compete on your computer via modem. The opponent is also hooked up to a computer and modem, but that opponent just may happen to be across town. You don't even have to know your opponent. Many computer games are starting to offer modem play. Local Bulletin Board Systems usually offer lists of players specializing in different modem games. Once you access such a list, you can play against anybody equipped with a modem and a copy of the game.

Meet Grunt, Rider, Boomer, Spy, and Comcen, your robots to command. The press of a space bar determines which player picks the game type and map. Game types run the gamut from scrimmage (for beginners or those who just want to play quick and dirty) to full war. Look out! The full war game enables you to deploy your grunts (bombers) and missiles (anti-grunts).

A neat feature is the Voice/Pause option, which you get when you're playing the game over the phone lines. You can pick up the phone and talk with your opponent, and during the conversation the game will pause. This is handy when neither of you have read the manual and don't know what to do next.

The manual recommends that you find a player equal in skill to yours. You can figure your average game score and then handicap lesser players to even things out a bit.

You can send messages to your enemy any time by just hitting the <Return> key. It's advisable to at least send a congratulatory message to the victor and a word of encouragement to the loser. Remarks like "Even my dog wouldn't do that" are not encouraged. Other games with modem play capabilities allow for on-line "chatting," or typing messages to each other.

On the more classical game front, another modem gaming software program features chess, checkers, and backgammon. *Teleplay* lets you sit down at the old cracker barrel for a rousing game of checkers, even if your opponent is miles away.

Teleplay is hard to play on an EGA screen because the chess pieces on the two sides are busy, and they're the same bright colors, just reversed. A plus is that you can send messages to your opponent, such as "What'd you do that for?" If things are really going badly, you can save the game for another day and go read up on what the great chessmasters would have done in your spot (of course, they never would have got into such a jam in the first place . . .).

Working From Home

You can access your work computer at home with the help of remote computer software. Remote software runs in the background of both the local and remote computer until called up with hot keys. Both the remote and host computer can initiate calls using the dialing directory included with most of these packages. While connected, you can print files, transfer files, or show someone at the remote computer how to work a particularly difficult command. With the surge in popularity of laptop computers, imagine being able to control your PC back at the office from your hotel room! Family vacations will never be the same.

One of the most convenient features offered by most remote software packages is the ability to record screen sequences within a session for playback later. You can even pause within a session to play back earlier transactions. This is great for training and system troubleshooting.

Banking From Home

If banking is inconvenient, or you just want to partake of the ultimate that high-tech has to offer, you can pay bills electronically without ever setting pen to paper. When you write a paper check to a merchant, it makes its way back to the bank, where the amount is manually entered into a computer and transmitted to the Federal Reserve. With check-writing programs, you enter and send your payment information directly to the Federal Reserve. Eliminate the middleman.

The plus is that it's safe, and the built-in check register keeps your account updated consistently. Tax time becomes a breeze. But there's always a minus—services like these are expensive.

Commercial On-Line Services

Accu-Weather Forecaster
Accu-Weather, Metacomet Software, P.O. Box 31337
Hartford, CT 06103, (800) 782-5661

CompuServe Information Service
CompuServe, Inc., 5000 Arlington Centre Blvd.
Columbus OH 43220, (614) 457-0802, (800) 848-8199

Connect Professional Information Network
Connect, Inc.1, 0101 Bubb Road
Cupertino, CA 95014, (408) 973-0110, (800) 262-2638

DASnet Service
DA Systems, Inc., 1503 E. Campbell Avenue
Campbell, CA 95008, (408) 559-7434

Dialog
Dialog Information Services, Inc., 3460 Hillview Avenue
Palo Alto, CA 94304, (415) 858-2700, (800) 334-2564

Dow Jones News/Retrieval
Dow Jones & Company, Inc., P.O. Box 300
Princeton, NJ 08543, (609) 520-4641

GEnie
General Electric Information Services, 401 N. Washington Street
Rockville, MD 20850, (301) 340-4000, (800) 638-9600

Lexis/Nexis
Mead Data Central, 9443 Springsboro Pike, P.O. Box 933
Dayton, OH 45401, (800) 227-4908

MCI Mail
MCI Mail, 1150 17th Street NW, 8th Floor
Washington, DC 20036, (202) 833-8484, (800) 444-6245

NewsNet, Inc.
NewsNet, Inc., 945 Haverford Road
Bryn Mawr, PA 19010, (215) 527-8030, (800) 345-1301

Prodigy Services
(800) Prodigy
(Free start-up kits are usually available)

The Source
Source Telecomputing, 1616 Anderson Road, P.O. Box 1305
McLean, VA 22101, (703) 821-6666, (800) 336-3366

Sources for Telecommunications Software

IBM-Compatibles Telecommunications Software

Boyan 4.0 ($55)
Boyan Communications, 9458 Two Hills Court
Columbia, MD 21045-3228, (919) 682-4225 (BBS)

Crosstalk Communicator 3.8, ($195)
Crosstalk Mk.4 1.1 ($245)
DCA/Crosstalk Communications, 1000 Holcomb Woods Pkwy.
Roswell, CA 30076, (404) 442-4930, (404) 740-8428 (BBS)

Mirror III ($149)
SoftKlone Distributing Corp., 327 Office Plaza Drive, Suite 100
Tallahassee, FL 32301, (904) 878-8564, (904) 878-9884 (BBS)

Microphone for Windows ($250)
Software Ventures Corp., 2907 Claremont Avenue, Suite 220
Berkeley, CA 94705, (800) 336-6477

ProComm Plus ($68.99)
Datastorm Technologies
(Retail outlets everywhere)

Qmodem SST 4.0 ($45; manual $15)
The Forbin Project, Inc., P.O. Box 702
Cedar Falls, IA 50613, (319) 266-0543, (319) 266-0540 (BBS)

Relay Gold 5.0 ($299)
Microcom Software Division, 41 Kenosia Avenue
Danbury, CT 06810-9990, (800) 847-3529, (203) 798-3800

Smartcomm III 2.0 ($199)
Hayes Microcomputer Products, Inc., P.O. Box 105203
Atlanta, GA 30348, (404) 441-1617, (800) 847-2937 (BBS)

IBM-Compatible Connectivity Software

Laplink Pro
($169.95, File Transfer; IBM-compatible desktops and laptops)
Traveling Software, Inc., 18702 North Creek Parkway
Bothell, WA 98011, (800) 343-8080

Macintosh Telecommunications Software

MicroPhone II
($295, Telecommunications; Macintosh 512KE or larger)
Software Ventures Corp., 2907 Claremont Avenue, Suite 220
Berkeley, CA 94705, (800) 336-6477

White Knight
($139, Telecommunications; Macintosh 512K and larger)
FreeSoft, 150 Hickory Drive
Beaver Falls, PA 15010, (412) 846-2700

Smartcom II for the Mac
($149, Terminal Emulation; any Macintosh)
Hayes Microcomputer Products, Inc., P.O. Box 105203
Atlanta, GA 30348, (404) 449-8791

Quick Link II ($95, Telecommunications; Mac 512K and larger)
Smith Micro Software, Inc., P.O. Box 7137
Huntington Beach, CA 92615, (714) 964-0412

Connectivity Software

MacBlast ($195, Asynchronous File Transfer; Mac Plus or larger)
Communications Research Group, 5615 Corporate Blvd.
Baton Rouge, LA 70808, (504) 923-0888, or (800) 242-5278

MacLinkPlus
($199, File Transfer and Translation; Mac Plus or larger)
Data Viz, Inc., 35 Corporate Drive
Trumbull, CT 06611, (203) 268-0030

ProLink ($59.95, File Transfer; Apple II and Macintosh)
Alsoft, Inc., P.O. Box 927
Spring, TX 77383, (713) 353-4090

Modem Gaming Software

Modem Wars ($39.95)
Electronic Arts, P.O. Box 7578
San Mateo, CA 94403-7578, (415) 572-2787

TelePlay ($19.95)
Teletronics, Inc., 3368 Governor Drive, Suite F-252
San Diego, CA 92122

Remote Access Software

Carbon Copy Plus, $195
Microcom, 500 River Ridge Drive
Norwood, MA 02062-5028, (617) 551-1999

pcAnywhere III ($140, IBM-compatibles)
Dynamic Microprocessor Associates, Inc., 60 E. 42nd Street
New York, NY 10165

Modem Banking Software

CheckFree ($49.95, IBM-compatibles)
CheckFree Technologies, P.O. Box 897
Columbus, OH 43216, (614) 898-6000

Appendix A

Shareware Isn't Scareware

Most shareware and public domain programs discussed in this book come on a single diskette, without any fancy packaging or manuals. This is a mixed blessing.

These no-frills programs can be distributed cheaply (or for free, in the case of public domain software). On the other hand, some people feel intimidated without manuals and packaging to assist them in becoming familiar with the software. Especially if they have a DOS-based computer.

No need for alarm. It's easy to get up and running with a new shareware diskette. If you have an IBM-compatible computer, just follow these easy steps, and you'll be neck-deep in shareware before you know it.

Simply insert the diskette into your floppy drive (probably Drive A), change to drive A by typing "A:", then type "DIR" to get a directory of the diskette's contents.

Note: If the program is large, and the diskette's contents scroll by while you watch helplessly, type "DIR/P" instead. That will give you the directory a Page at a time. Another directory favorite is "DIR/W" which gives you a Wide directory—a directory set up in columns—taking up less space while letting you see everything at once. This last is recommended for DOS gurus only, since the display doesn't clearly differentiate between file names and subdirectories.)

By now you've typed "DIR" and the contents of the shareware diskette are up there on the screen. It's easy to tell what the files in the program do—just look at their extensions. Extensions are those three letters that come after the period in a file name. For example, in a file named WP.EXE, the extension is "EXE". Following is a list of the most common, and important, extensions and what they do.

File Extensions and Their Functions

EXE
This stands for "executable" file and runs the program. Type what comes before EXE and press the <Enter> key; the program should start up. For example, if the filename were BASEBALL.EXE, type "BASEBALL" at the prompt and the program will start running.

COM
This stands for "command" file, and will run the program. Type what comes before COM, press the <Enter> key, and the program should run.

BAT
This stands for "batch" file, which someone has written to make starting up the program or printing documentation easier. Type what comes before BAT and press the <Enter> key.

BAS
This stands for "BASIC" and you must be in the BASIC program that came with your computer in order to run a program with this extension.

DOC, or TXT
These stand for documentation files, and you may access this important information in two ways. You could type "TYPE WHAT-EVER.DOC" (replacing "WHATEVER" with the actual file name), but you'd have to keep pressing <Ctrl-S> to get it to stop scrolling down your screen so quickly you can't read it. Or you can type "LIST WHATEVER.DOC" if you have the handy utility *LIST* on your hard drive. Be sure to read the DOC or TXT file *before* running the program.

READ.ME
If you see any variation of this filename on the program diskette, first type "TYPE READ.ME" or "LIST READ.ME" (if you have the *LIST* utility mentioned above), before doing anything

else—especially trying to run the actual program. Chances are this file contains last-minute information crucial to getting the program running.

ARC

This stands for "ARChived" file and means that the entire program is hiding in here with all of its various files compressed, or archived, into one neat package. (Computer programmers are into neatness.) The diskette probably contains a decompression or unarchiving utility, probably called PKXARC.COM or PKUN-PAK.CTL. If these programs are there, to unarchive the program, stick a blank, formatted diskette in your B: drive, and type "PKXARC PROGRAM B:" (substitute the actual file name for the word "PROGRAM" here). Magically, the program will decompress onto the diskette in drive b:, and instead of one big file you'll have several. If you have a hard disk, it's recommended to make a special subdirectory there just for unarchiving and trying out new shareware programs. I call mine "JUNK". That way, I can type "PKXARC PROGRAM C:\JUNK" and all the program's files go obediently to JUNK, where they're easy to identify and keep separate from the other programs on my hard disk. And if I don't like the program, I just type "DEL C:\JUNK *.*" and it's gone.

Of course, you'll see many other file extensions on program diskettes, but these are the basics and ought to get you going.

Appendix B

The World of CD-ROM

Imagine a pile of thousands of floppy disks, packed full with tens of thousands of shareware programs. Wouldn't it be fun to have all those disks and programs at once? Think of all the interesting hobby and household applications hiding in these disks. Storing and accessing them all could be a mess, though, unless you're a supremely organized being.

Now, imagine being able to keep all those programs on your computer, ready for use at the press of a key. Sound impossible? The marvels of computer compact disc technology, or CD-ROM, make accessing any program quick and easy.

The real advantage to having CD-ROM (Compact Disc–Read Only Memory) is that CD-ROM discs are able to store much more information than floppy or even hard disks.

So, although you can only read from them and not write information to them (as the name Read–Only Memory implies), a typical CD-ROM disc can hold about 550 megabytes, or the equivalent of about 1,565 of the older 360K MS-DOS diskettes, 700 of the newer, double-sided 3½-inch diskettes, or 10 55-MB hard disks.

Think of CD-ROM discs as a kind of publishing medium, but one where the information is in computer-readable form ready to be copied over into any of your normal computer applications. (And, a CD-ROM disc is easier to tuck in your pocket than 1,565 diskettes!)

What's Available on CD-ROM?

At first, commercial CD-ROM discs focused on information useful mostly to corporations, financial whizzes, and libraries. CD-ROM discs can easily handle huge databases, since they have such large capacities. But now, more and more publishers are putting out CD-ROM discs of interest to the home user. There's even a magazine devoted solely to new CD-ROM products and developments: *CD-ROM Review*.

Microsoft Bookshelf

Crowded onto one CD-ROM disc are all the programs a student or writer could ever want. *Bookshelf* features *The American Heritage Dictionary*, *Roget's II Electronic Thesaurus*, *Bartlett's Familiar Quotations*, the *Chicago Manual of Style*, the *Houghton Mifflin Spelling Verifier and Corrector*, the *Houghton Mifflin Usage Alert*, *The World Almanac and Book of Facts* (for the current year), the *U.S. Zip Code Directory*, *Business Information Sources*, and a collection of business and personal forms and letters.

Bookshelf's most attractive feature is that it's RAM resident, so it can pop up in the middle of your favorite word processor or other application. I enjoyed typing an address in a *WordPerfect* letter, pressing a key, and seeing *Bookshelf* zap in the zip code.

The PC-SIG Library on CD-ROM

Wow! The *PC-SIG Library on CD-ROM* disc is stuffed with every single shareware and public domain program distributed by PC-SIG, the Silicon Valley company that pioneered the concept of shareware in the early days of the PC and who keep the world's largest library of shareware programs. (See Appendix A for a discussion of shareware.)

With this disc, you can access, copy to a hard disk or a floppy, and run powerful business programs, personal productivity tools, educational programs, programming tools, home software you've seen mentioned in other chapters in this book, games, and even desktop publishing software.

A plus: The CD-ROM disc comes with a 432-page book, *The Encyclopedia of Shareware*, so you can browse in bed and decide which programs to play with next.

Oxford English Dictionary

Did you ever get suckered into joining the Book of the Month Club just so you could buy the compact edition of the *Oxford*

English Dictionary (*OED*) for $25 instead of $250? Did you regret ordering it once you found out you had to use a magnifying glass to read it? Here's where CD-ROM technology really shines.

Available in a two-disc set, the CD-ROM *Oxford English Dictionary* lets you call up any word, whether obscure or everyday (talk about in-depth: this dictionary devotes seven pages to the word "what"). You can simply find out what it means or read further to learn the word's origin.

The best feature of the *OED* is that each entry contains several passages showing how the word's usage has evolved through the ages. If the word really intrigues you, you can even trace related or opposite words. Best of all, you can copy any passage into whatever document you want.

The Electronic Whole Earth Catalog

You may or may not be familiar with the *Whole Earth Catalog*, a book listing resources on almost every field of interest under the sun, first published in 1968 by Stewart Brand. When it first came out, the book was hailed by counter-culture types for its democratic and "you can do anything yourself" attitude.

The latest book version weighs more than $5\frac{1}{2}$ pounds, so the publishers decided to offer the catalog in electronic form (for Macintosh computers). The CD-ROM resource contains more than 3,500 entries on many subjects—from building your own home, managing and operating a small business, beekeeping, blacksmithing, your body and well-being—even computers.

Better than a book, the CD-ROM disc features cross-referencing, sound, and visuals. For example, users can actually listen to excerpts from more than 700 recordings, from blues to jazz to bird calls. Full-screen digitized images and more than 3,000 graphics are included, as well.

What You Need to Get Started With CD-ROM

The components of a CD-ROM setup include the CD-ROM disc, a CD-ROM drive unit, a disc caddie, a controller card, a cable, and a few manuals. And, of course, your computer.

The CD-ROM Disc, or Software

First of all, you'll need a CD-ROM disc. Find a disc on a topic or field of interest to you, because at $295-plus, the CD-ROM disc you choose should last awhile.

The CD-ROM Drive, or Hardware

The primary piece of hardware needed to "play" a CD-ROM disc is a CD-ROM drive. CD-ROM drives come in both external and internal forms, just like modems. Because they cost so much more than any other computer accessory, however, your best bet is to buy an external CD-ROM drive. That way, you don't have to worry about incompatibility in case you ever want to buy a new computer from a different computer family. If, for example, you decided to switch from a Macintosh computer to an IBM-compatible, you'd only have to replace the CD-ROM drive's controller card and cable—much less expensive than replacing the whole drive unit.

The external CD-ROM drive looks like a half-height computer box, but in place of a floppy disk drive there's a CD-ROM slot. Don't stick the CD-ROM disc right into the slot, however. Instead, slip the disc carefully into the removable disc caddie included with the drive. Then close the caddie and push it part way into the drive's slot, which grabs it and automatically inserts the caddie the rest of the way into the slot. When you want to quit your CD-ROM session, just press the Eject button under the slot, and the disc caddie pops out, ready to be loaded with another disc.

Included with the external CD-ROM drive is a CD-ROM controller card, which fits into an empty slot in your computer. Once it's snapped into place, a cable connects the controller card in your computer to the CD-ROM drive. It's important to make sure you have the correct interface cable for both the controller card and your model of CD-ROM drive. The CD-ROM drive also comes with an AC power cord, ready to take up yet another slot on your computer's power strip.

Now all the hardware is in place. But one crucial aspect is still missing. Your computer needs software to tell it there's a CD-ROM drive hooked up to it. (You'd think the computer would notice this intruder on its own, but it doesn't.)

This software varies, depending on what type of computer you own. One CD-ROM software package that performs this function for IBM-compatible computers is published by Microsoft. It's called "MS-DOS CD-ROM Extensions." For the Macintosh family of computers, an INIT file comes with the CD-ROM hardware and this tells the Mac to treat the CD-ROM drive like any other disk drive.

If you have an IBM-compatible computer, you'll probably need to add lines in your computer's CONFIG.SYS and AUTOEXEC.BAT files, telling your computer to look for the alien drive each time it boots up. The manuals and other user documentation that come with the drive and individual discs are very thorough, however, so you shouldn't have any trouble if you read these carefully before attempting installation.

Sources for CD-ROM Products

CD-ROM Review ($35/year)
CW Communications/Peterborough, P.O. Box 921
Farmingdale, NY 11737-9621

Bookshelf ($250)
Microsoft Corporation, 16011 NE 36th Way, P.O. Box 97017
Redmond WA 98073-9717, (206) 882-8080

PC-SIG CD-ROM ($149)
PC-SIG, 1030 East Duane Avenue, Suite D
Sunnyvale, CA 94086
(800) 222-2996 (CA), (800) 245-6717 (USA), (408) 730-9291

Educorp Macintosh Shareware CD-ROM ($199)
Educorp, 531 Stevens Avenue, Suite B
Solana Beach, CA 92075, (800) 843-9497, (619) 259-0255

Oxford English Dictionary ($1250)
TriStar Publishing, 475 Virginia Drive
Fort Washington, PA 19034, (215) 641-9600

The Electronic Whole Earth Catalog ($149.95)
Broderbund Software, Inc., 17 Paul Drive
San Rafael, CA 94903-2101, (415) 492-3200

The Sony Corporation
2132A East Dominguez Street
Carson, CA 90810

Amdek Corp.
3471 North First Street, Bldg. 3
San Jose, CA 95134, (408) 436-8570

Index

Other Books From
Computer Publishing Enterprises:

PC Secrets
Tips and Tricks to Increase Your Computer's Power
by R. Andrew Rathbone

Future Computer Opportunities
Visions of Computers Into the Year 2000
by Jack Dunning

Software Buying Secrets
by Wally Wang

DOS Secrets
by Dan Gookin

101 Computer Business Ideas
by Wally Wang

Digital Dave's Computer Tips and Secrets
A Beginner's Guide to Problem Solving
by Roy Davis

The Best FREE Time-Saving Utilities for the PC
by Wally Wang

How to Get Started With Modems
by Jim Kimble

How to Make Money With Computers
by Jack Dunning

Rookie Programming
A Newcomer's Guide to Programming in BASIC, C, and Pascal
by Ron Dippold

Hundreds of Fascinating and Unique Ways to Use Your Computer
by Tina Rathbone

The Computer Gamer's Bible
by R. Andrew Rathbone

Beginner's Guide to DOS
by Dan Gookin

Computer Entrepreneurs
People Who Built Successful Businesses Around Computers
by Linda Murphy

How to Understand and Buy Computers
By Dan Gookin

Parent's Guide to Educational Software and Computers
by Lynn Stewart and Toni Michael

The Official Computer Widow's (and Widower's) Handbook
by Experts on Computer Widow/Widowerhood

For more information about these books, call 1-800-544-5541.